Delinquent

How the American Juvenile Justice System is Failing Black Children

Daphne R. Robinson, JD, MPH

Delinquent

Published by Daphne R. Robinson in Partnership with
The Literary Revolutionary

THE LITERARY REVOLUTIONARY & Co

www.theliteraryrevolutionary.com

Editing By: Anjé McLish
Cover Design By: Ikuborije Opeyemi

Disclaimer:
I have tried to recreate events, locales and conversations
from my memories of them. In order to maintain their
anonymity, I have changed the names of individuals and
places. I may have changed some identifying
characteristics and details such as physical properties,
ages, and places of residence.

Manufactured in the United States of America

ISBN #: 978-1-950279-20-3
Library of Congress Control Number: 2020918033

Follow @daphne_r_robinson on Instagram!

Delinquent
How the American Juvenile Court is Failing Black Children

By:
Daphne R. Robinson, JD, MPH

Delinquent

Dedication

I dedicate this book to my parents, Eddie and Canary Robinson. As of this writing, they are still with me at ages 90 and 86, respectively. They have been the greatest parents and my biggest fans. They continue to encourage me and remind me that I can do all things through Christ who strengthens me.

The bulk of this book was written from a hospital bed after I suffered significant injuries in a motor vehicle accident in 2019. Without question, I could not have physically or mentally endured that life altering event without my three wonderful brothers, my sister, and some great friends. Their generosity in my time of need will never be forgotten.

Delinquent

Acknowledgements

I'd like to take this opportunity to acknowledge my friend and mentor, Judge James Stewart, Sr. When I left law school, I never dreamed that I'd become a prosecutor. I envisioned myself a public defender, championing the causes of the poor and downtrodden. But, one day in early 1993, while unemployed and living in Louisiana, I received a call from the office of State District Court Judge James E. Stewart, Sr. His secretary Roxanne Williams had a lovely voice and a warm personality that just oozed through the telephone. She told me that Judge Stewart wanted to interview me for a job as his law clerk at the First Judicial District Court. I needed a job at the time, so I gladly agreed to the interview and made my way to meet with him. The Judge had been a prosecutor for many years in Louisiana, and extolled the virtues of the profession. That was 27 years ago. I never dreamed that in 2020 he'd be an elected DA and I'd work for him once again. I owe him more than I can ever repay.

Delinquent

Daphne R. Robinson

Table of Contents

Delinquent

1

How Did I Get Here?

While sitting in the kitchen of the District Attorney's Office feeling like a fish in a fishbowl, people passing by the kitchen door peering in at me as if I could not hear or see them as they passed, a part of me was relieved that I had already packed up my office. I did that the day after the new DA was sworn in. The rumor swirled for months that I would be one of the first people to be fired if Phillip was elected. People often ask me why I was the first lawyer fired (I certainly wasn't the last; many others followed). I tell them that I'm sure there were a variety of reasons. But, I believe one of the most significant reasons was my vocal concern and growing resentment about the inequities that I saw in the juvenile justice system after over 20 years as an African-American female prosecutor in that system.

The newly elected DA appeared at the door of the kitchen and told me to meet him in the library. It was my turn. When I look back on it, the act of being fired – an act that changed my life – took less than 10 minutes. I sat down at the conference table and in the room were the First Assistant, the Office Administrator, and the DA. Once I sat down, the new DA said, "We have decided to go in a different direction. We appreciate your service." That's it. "Twenty years of service and that's it," I thought. Fighting back tears, I rose, said thank you, shook the hand of each person seated at the table, walked out the door and went directly to my car, piled to the brim with files, documents, and plaques of days gone by.

Although scared to death about what the future would hold for me, I felt an incredible sense of relief. I tell people that I felt like a 100 pound weight had been lifted from my shoulders. I was finally free ... free to tell my story as an African American woman, who has prosecuted hundreds, if not thousands, of juvenile cases for more than 25 years in multiple jurisdictions in Louisiana, the incarceration capital of the world. It is my sincere hope that this book will create a dialogue about how vulnerable populations, in this case, children of color, are treated in the juvenile justice system. They suffer in ways that are distinctly different from adults in the criminal justice system, and it is important that we acknowledge that fact.

When I found myself waiting to be fired, I asked myself, "How did I get here?" Like most professional, single women in their late 40's that I knew, I was the classic overachiever. I graduated summa cum laude from Tougaloo College, a historically black college in Jackson, Mississippi.

Daphne R. Robinson

After college, I attended the American University Washington College of Law in Washington, D.C. and received a Juris Doctorate Degree in 1991. My first job after law school was law clerk to a federal judge in Louisiana. After that, I worked for state district court judges and an appellate court judge in Shreveport, Louisiana. I briefly worked as an assistant district attorney in New Orleans as a juvenile prosecutor, and later returned to Alexandria, Louisiana in 1996 to serve as the chief assistant district attorney in the juvenile division. In my mind, I had done all of the right things. By the time I sat in that kitchen, keenly aware of my fate, I had practiced law in Louisiana for well over 25 years, owned my own home, and enjoyed a good reputation in the community as an attorney and a community leader.

I grew up in the Mississippi Delta, the distinctive northwest section of the state, which lies between the Mississippi and Yazoo Rivers. The region has been called "the most southern place on earth," because of its unique racial, cultural, and economic history. It is 200 miles long and 87 miles across at its widest point. It encompasses approximately 4,415,000 acres, or, some 7,000 square miles of alluvial floodplain.[1] It's known as some of the richest land outside of the Nile River Valley, but it also bears a painful history of slavery and Jim Crow. In so many ways, the vestiges of racism and sanctioned apartheid in the Mississippi Delta have hobbled the educational and economic attainment of folks of color in the region to this day.

As an African-American female growing up in one of the most impoverished areas in the country, I was not supposed to succeed. I was supposed to be a statistic – pregnant by the age of 16, uneducated, and living on public assistance. That was supposed to be my destiny. After all, between 1980 and 1990, 70.5 out of 1,000 females between the ages of 15 and 17 in the state of Mississippi became pregnant. At the time, this was one of the highest rates of teenage pregnancy in the country.[2] And sadly, these same statistics for African-American females in the Mississippi, Louisiana, and Arkansas Delta, where I grew up, have not improved significantly. Despite teen pregnancy rates declining across the country, Mississippi still ranked third highest in the nation for teen birth rates as late as 2016.[3] Like many women, particularly women of color growing up in the deep South or the inner city, I overcame a predetermined destiny just to graduate from high school, attend college, and eventually law school.

So, you can imagine my dismay as I sat in that kitchen in January of 2015 contemplating my fate. I had never in my entire life been fired from a job. I was always the person who came to work early when it was necessary and stayed late most days. In almost twenty years of working in that office, I had received many accolades from those inside and outside of the legal system. One of my greatest accomplishments while working in the DA's Office was garnering the recognition of the John T. and Catherine D. MacArthur Foundation for my efforts in reducing the rate of juvenile crime in the

Daphne R. Robinson

jurisdiction. But, sadly, what I learned was that nothing I did to reduce the rate of juvenile crime or to raise the awareness of the public about crime and juvenile justice mattered. As an African American female in a system dominated by Southern white men, I was supposed to be silent, remain in my place, and be grateful because I enjoyed the spoils of a profession and position that only white males were to enjoy. And I was supposed to be complicit through my silence about a system that treats black children as disposable and is failing our youth on a daily basis. Michelle Alexander, the author of the **New Jim Crow: Mass Incarceration in the Age of Colorblindness**, and the inspiration for this book, wrote, "[T]hroughout our history, there have been African Americans who, for a variety of reasons, have defended or been complicit with the prevailing system of control."[4] As a prosecutor, who is well aware of the risks posed by crime, particularly violent crime, I do believe that juveniles should be held accountable for the harm caused to unwitting victims and families. However, I refuse to continue to defend or support the current state of juvenile justice or continue to be complicit in its perpetual failure to nurture, protect, and rehabilitate youth of color.

The question becomes for whom am I writing this book. Truthfully, I am writing this book for myself and other people like me -- fair-minded people working in the system, who know that it is built on a foundation of historical, institutional racism in which 'rules, regulations, norms, laws, discourses, and procedures ... account for

15

pernicious and racialized differential treatment and outcomes'[5] for black children. Some maintain that such an argument diminishes the role of individual actors, like judges, prosecutors, public defenders and probation officers in maintaining the system of racism. I agree that we cannot discount the role that implicit bias, and in some cases, overt racial discrimination, play in the juvenile justice system to this day. It has even been shown that black folks, as well as white folks, working in the system hold negative attitudes and beliefs about children of color, which in turn can impact their expectations and actions towards children of color.[6] For years, I tried to convince myself that because I was fair and just, I could make the system fair and just. What I learned was that not only is the system unfair and unjust to children of color, it can be completely indifferent to their particular needs and experiences. The current system of juvenile justice in this country does not need racial hostility or overt bigotry to handicap children, it only needs racial indifference.[7]

But, as activists for juvenile justice reform working outside (and inside) the system, I want this book to confirm for you what you already know and to convince you that we must all tell the *complete* story when discussing the plight of black children in the system. Don't just stand by and let the story be told that Jakori committed a robbery. The end. It's always more than that. The complete story is that Jakori's parents are incarcerated; he's living with an elderly grandmother in a neighborhood surrounded by crime and drugs; he's been in special ed classes all of his life; he's 15 and still in the 6th grade; and he's been expelled from school before the school year really started. Telling the complete story removes the veil of indifference that police, judges, public defenders, and prosecutors wear. Knowing the complete story forces stakeholders in the system to make sound decisions that take into account the whole child and not just the sum total of his delinquent actions.

Although I use the terms black boys, black girls, or children of color interchangeably throughout these pages, I should clarify *about whom* I am writing this book. I have tried to be as balanced as possible in this account of black children caught up in the American juvenile court. I didn't want to talk exclusively about black boys or black girls, but about *black children*, because it is *black children*, who, regardless of gender, are far more likely than their white counterparts, to be represented at every stage of the juvenile justice process.

2

The History of the Juvenile Justice System and Children of Color

Any exploration of the juvenile justice system and its current impact on children of color would be incomplete without an examination of this country's initial response to the needs of black children.

The first people of African descent were brought to this country 400 years ago to Jamestown, Virginia. At the time, there were no laws in the colonies that permitted slavery, so the Africans were initially treated like indentured servants. Indentured servants typically worked four to seven years in exchange for passage, room, board, lodging and freedom dues. While the life of an indentured servant was harsh and restrictive, it wasn't slavery. Although indentured servants had some rights, their lives were still difficult.[8]

Eventually, laws sanctioning slavery passed in 1661 in Virginia, and the bondage of the Africans in Jamestown as indentured servants was later converted to a lifetime of enslavement that was passed on from generation to generation.[9] By 1860, the population of enslaved people increased to 3,952,760, fifty-six percent (56%) of whom were under the age of 20.[10] This meant that the children of slaves were born into slavery, and thus had to endure the brutalities of the system as well. Little regard was paid by slave owners to keeping families together. Children were seen as simply commodities to be exploited and sold.[11]

Instructions given by masters to overseers regarding punishment rarely if ever discriminated in favor of child slaves, and from this it can be assumed that children were subject to the same harsh treatments as were adults. The prevailing general assumption of the age of 'spare the rod and spoil the child' appears to have been applied even more stringently to slave children who were also being trained for a life of servitude. They might be whipped or even required to swallow worms they failed to pick off cotton or tobacco plants. During adolescence, a majority of slave youth were sold or hired away. Children experienced beatings of one kind or another and certainly witnessed the beating of adults, their parents, and their peers. Child slaves had to quickly come to terms with the concept of pain and punishment as an everyday fact of their lives. Those who failed to absorb this aspect of suffering and reacted by running away were often seen as "spirited", and whose spirit had to be broken.[12] This begins the history of the social control and objectification of black children in this country.

Until recently, the subject of childhood under slavery was almost entirely unstudied. This was true despite the fact that childhood is central to an understanding of slavery. In classical antiquity, abandoned children were a major source of slaves. Although most sub-Saharan Africans forced into slavery were in their teens and 20s, a substantial and growing proportion were children. In the American South in the decades before the Civil War, half of all slaves were under 16.[13]

A focus on children not only underscores slavery's oppressions, it also reveals the ways that enslaved children and their parents dealt with slavery's hardships and horrors. The study of slave children has brought many important facts to light. Infant and child mortality rates were twice as high among slave children as among southern white children. A major contributor to the high infant and child death rate was chronic undernourishment.[14] Slave owners showed surprisingly little concern for slave mothers' health or diet during pregnancy, providing pregnant women with no extra rations and employing them in intensive field work even in the last week before they gave birth. Not surprisingly, slave mothers suffered high rates of spontaneous abortions, stillbirths, and deaths shortly after birth. Half of all slave infants weighed less than 5.5 pounds at birth, or what we would today consider to be severely underweight.[15]

Growth rates among slave children were extremely slow. Most infants were weaned early, within three or four months of birth, and then fed gruel or porridge made of cornmeal. Around the age of three, they began to eat vegetables, soups, potatoes, molasses, grits, hominy, and cornbread. This diet lacked protein, thiamine, niacin, calcium, magnesium, and vitamin D, and as a result, slave children often suffered from night blindness, abdominal swellings, swollen muscles, bowed legs, skin lesions, and convulsions. These apparently stemmed from beriberi, pellagra, tetany, rickets, and kwashiorkor, diseases that are caused by protein and nutritional deficiencies.[16] Deprived of an adequate diet, slave children were very small by modern standards.

About half of all U.S. slave children grew up apart from their father, either because he lived on another plantation, had been sold away, or was white. On large plantations, infants and very young children were supervised and cared for by adults other than their parents. Children as young as two or three might work at domestic chores, including childcare or collecting trash and kindling, carrying water, scaring away birds, weeding, or plucking grubs from plants. Generally, in the U.S. South, children entered field work between the ages of 8 and 12.[17]

As the country grappled with the possibility of emancipating the roughly 4,000,000 slaves in this country and headed towards the brink of Civil War, some who considered themselves abolitionists or well-meaning politicians such as President Abraham Lincoln believed that once the slaves were freed, they should be recolonized in Africa. In 1862, Abraham Lincoln called a meeting of well-respected black clergymen. He explained that Congress had appropriated a sum of money for the expatriation of black people, once emancipated, back to Africa because he, among others, was of the belief that once freed, black and white people could not live together in this country peacefully. Although the clergymen invited to the meeting left agreeing to consider the proposal, nothing ever came of the idea because black people considered America their own country, and what they wanted was freedom and equality here.[18] This kind of discourse fueled the white supremacist theories of the day that black people and their children were morally and intellectually inferior to white people.

3

Systemic Racism Embedded into the Juvenile Justice System

The racial bondage of black children is embedded into the juvenile justice system to this day. Even those who dared to create a juvenile justice system for the benefit of children, still created a two-tiered system in which black children were considered less than white children and were treated accordingly. Geoff K. Ward wrote in his book, ***The Black Child-Savers***, "Race-based distinction was, thus, sewn into the original fabric of twentieth-century juvenile justice systems, its seam being defined by the stark, if unstable, divide between progressive child-welfare ideals and evolving structures of American apartheid."[19]

After the end of chattel slavery in the South, there grew convict leasing. This was the practice in which states like Mississippi would loan out its black prison population to work on plantations and build railroads.[20] In Mississippi, there was no distinction between punishing children and punishing adults.[21] Because the growth of the juvenile justice movement peaked during the same period that encompassed emancipation, Reconstruction, and the era of Jim Crow laws and policies, black children and families were marginalized and excluded from the building of the American juvenile justice system.

In the early 19th century, new facilities began to open to help control troubled, wayward or orphaned children. The purpose of this movement was to discontinue the use of adult jails or almshouses (locked one room buildings) that housed adults and children with a myriad of problems. The first such institution for delinquent children in the United States in 1824 was called the New York House of Refuge.[22] It was the first institution of its kind designed to house poor, destitute and vagrant youth, who were deemed by authorities to be on the path towards delinquency. The House of Refuge was seen as a humane approach to housing children in difficult circumstances. However, it should be noted that black children were initially excluded from these efforts.[23]

A decade later, black children were allowed admission to the House of Refuge, but only in special sections for 'colored children.'[24] Black children admitted to the houses of refuge were, on the average, one and a half to two years younger than the average white children of the same gender, while also enduring longer sentences and harsher treatment. They also suffered a disproportionately higher death rate in these facilities, and upon discharge could look to fewer opportunities for advancement than their White counterparts.[25] In the deep South, the first House of Refuge was opened in New Orleans in 1847.[26] The facility is said to have done little more than separate younger offenders from older offenders and was, of course, exclusively for white children.[27]

It was in this milieu of racial oppression of black people, that the first juvenile court was created in this country in Chicago, Illinois, in 1899. This was seen as a victory by progressives or 'child savers' in the country because it firmly established that the problems of juveniles were distinct from those of adults and as a result, there should be separate courts for the both groups. But, sadly, the historical narratives of the first juveniles to pass through the early juvenile court have primarily focused on the experiences of white and immigrant children and not the experiences of black children.[28]

The early years of the first juvenile court coincided with the First and Second World Wars and the Great Migration, the period of time that spanned from 1910 to 1945, in which 1.5 million African Americans moved from the deep South to the North to find greater economic opportunity and to escape the tyranny of white supremacy.[29] However, the mass movement of African Americans from the rural South to large cities like Chicago and New York, ignited racial tensions across the North as well.

In her book, *The Criminalization of Black Children: Race, Gender, and Delinquency in*

Chicago's Juvenile Justice System, Tera Eva Agyepong contends that black children were marked as delinquent even before they entered the juvenile justice system.[30] Black children were often classified as delinquent, meaning they committed a criminal act, when they more accurately should have been labeled as dependent.[31] Under the law at the time, a child was determined to be dependent "☐if he or she were orphaned or did not have safe or appropriate parental care due to abuse, neglect, abandonment, or extreme poverty."[32] To illustrate the point, the author tells the story of 'Mary Tripplett.' Mary, an eleven-year-old black female, was an orphan from Memphis, Tennessee in 1899, whose mother was deceased and whose father had recently left the state.[33] Mary was brought to court by Elizabeth McDonald, the only black female probation officer at the time, because she felt that the child needed help.[34] Although the probation officer noted in the petition that Mary was a dependent child, the matter was filed on a delinquent petition form. This purported type of 'clerical error' labeled Mary a delinquent child and many other black children who should have been categorized as dependent in the first juvenile court from 1899 to 1945.[35]

Agyepong argues in her book, and I agree, that labeling black children as delinquent or criminal and white children as dependent or needy ultimately racialized the categories and began the trend of criminalizing black children. I can recall numerous instances in my own professional career as a prosecutor that I was asked by people inside and outside of the system, to assist a white child by changing a serious delinquent charge, such as burglary or sexual assault, to a dependent charge. The person asking was often unrelated to the child. But, rarely, have I been asked to do the same for a black child.

In 2019, Misty, a 15-year-old white female, was charged with the murder of an Arab American store owner. The victim was stabbed to death by the child and her adult sibling. The body was doused with gasoline and set on fire, and the two girls fled to Florida in the victim's vehicle. They were later apprehended, and the 15-year-old was tried in juvenile court. In the early stages of the prosecution, I was sitting in a meeting when I heard discussions of reducing the charge to the equivalent of a dependency charge, because the juvenile offender had been previously abused by her biological parents and had been in and out of foster care. I was not sure if the person who raised the issue was serious or not; but before the discussion started heading down the wrong path, I quickly raised my hand and pointed out that if this same delinquent act had been committed by a 15-year-old black male, we would not have been having this discussion.

Race Forward: The Center for Racial Innovation (CRI), a non-profit racial justice organization based in Oakland, California, defines institutional racism as the unfair policies and discriminatory practices of particular institutions – schools, workplaces, the criminal justice system, the child welfare system – that routinely produce racially inequitable outcomes for people of color and advantages for white people.[36] CRI further defines structural racism as "racial bias among institutions and across society. It involves the cumulative and compounding effects of an array of societal factors including the history, culture, ideology and interactions of institutions and policies that systematically privilege white people and disadvantage people of color."[37]

Both concepts can be simply explained by using the metaphor of an iceberg, as described in the article "Structural Racism and Health Inequities" by Gilbert C. Gee and Chandra L. Ford.[38] An iceberg is a large piece of freshwater ice that has broken off a glacier and is floating in the open saltwater. The area that you can see above water is usually 3 to 200 feet above sea level and weighs over 100,000 metric tons. This area of the iceberg represents overt racial discrimination, such as cross burnings. Anyone can see it, and everyone knows to avoid it at all costs. However, over 90% of the iceberg's mass is still below the surface of the water. This area below the water represents the largest and most dangerous part of the iceberg because it is hidden out of sight and almost impossible to dismantle. This portion of the iceberg represents institutional and systemic racism.

Today, there is a different juvenile justice system in each state and the District of Columbia. Juvenile courts are governed by the various laws of each state and municipality in which they are located. Although juvenile courts across the country function independently of one another, an overrepresentation of African American children still exists at every stage of the juvenile justice process – from arrest to confinement – and is the direct result of institutional and structural racism. Although many of these courts may look diverse and inclusive "above the water" because there are black judges, black prosecutors, black public defenders, and black probation personnel, the massive, intractable portion of the iceberg that represents institutional and systemic racism still lies beneath the surface in the form of laws and policies.

According to data released by the Department of Justice in 2017, black youth were more than five times as likely to be detained or committed to juvenile facilities compared to white youth in 2015. This was a 22% increase from the year 2001.[39] In 2001, black youth were more than four times as likely to be detained or committed to juvenile facilities compared to white youth. Similarly, in Louisiana black youth were 4.75 times more likely to be detained or committed to juvenile facilities than white youth in 2015.[40] Juvenile facilities include residential treatment centers, detention centers, training schools, and juvenile jails and prisons across the country. Black children are more likely to be in custody in every state, except Hawaii.[41] These figures are particularly shocking when one takes into account that black children only make up 16% of the total number of children in the United States.[42] Overall, although the levels of youth incarceration have declined in the past few years, the levels of racial disparity when comparing black to white is quite stark.

The growing disparity in incarceration is believed to stem from the growing disparities in arrest rates. Arresting agencies – municipal, county, and state – are the funnel through which kids arrive at the juvenile justice system. Black children are more than twice as likely to be arrested than white children. Yet, statistics show that black and white children are just as likely to commit the same offenses, such as fighting at school, skipping glass, carrying weapons, using illicit substances or stealing.[43]

During the Obama administration, the Department of Education collected data from 72,000 schools across the country from the 2009 to 2010 school year.[44] The data indicated that 96,000 students were arrested and 242,000 were "referred" to law enforcement by school leaders, meaning the students were not necessarily arrested.[45] However, an overwhelming 70% percent of the students arrested were black or Latino males.[46]

In my years of practice, there were white children arrested, charged, and brought to court. I do not want to give anyone the impression that they were not. However, it is without question that the number of white children that I have prosecuted over the years is substantially lower than the number of black children that I have prosecuted. As a matter of fact, in Louisiana, I rarely saw white children come to delinquency court at all. When they did come to court, their cases were more likely to be diverted or reduced to status offenses without my input. The sighting of a white child in juvenile court was so rare that a new public defender assigned to the same court with me once remarked, "Do white kids commit crimes in this parish?" When I responded, "Of course, they do." She said, "Well, obviously they aren't arrested because I rarely see them in court."

4

How School Systems Contribute to the Delinquent Label

"As a single woman with no children, I admit that I know nothing about raising good children, but as a prosecutor who has worked in the juvenile justice system for 20 plus years, I can tell you exactly how to raise bad ones."

- Daphne Robinson

For more than a decade, the focus has been on the overrepresentation of children of color throughout every aspect of the juvenile justice system. However, for the purposes of this chapter, I want to discuss how the various systems that interact with children either prevent or contribute to their delinquent behavior. In public health, the socio-ecological model is a framework for understanding how behavior can be affected by the interaction of an individual with the various levels of society.[47]

Daphne R. Robinson

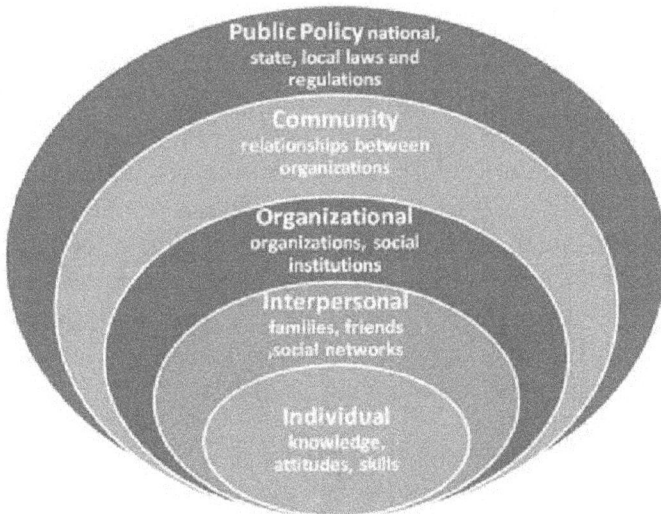

The model includes a nested diagram with labels: Public Policy (national, state, local laws and regulations), Community (relationships between organizations), Organizational (organizations, social institutions), Interpersonal (families, friends, social networks), Individual (knowledge, attitudes, skills).

The Socio-Ecological Model

The model includes five nested hierarchical levels: individual, interpersonal, community, organization, and policy.[48] When designing prevention and intervention programs for youth to prevent or reduce delinquent behavior, the most effective approaches use a combination of evidence-based interventions at all levels of the model.[49] However, rather than acting as networks and connections that foster and promote positive, protective factors for children, some levels are maladaptive and act as direct pathways to the juvenile justice system. This can be especially true of schools, which operate in the lives of children at the community level of the socio-ecological model.

Since the first large scale school shooting at Columbine High School in Columbine, Colorado in

1999, there has been a tremendous push by the nation's local law enforcement agencies to use precious state and federal resources to put police officers in schools and classrooms. The Office of Community Oriented Policing provided over 750 million in federal dollars for approximately 6,500 officers from 1999 to 2005 with much of the increase in funding to that office occurring after Columbine.[50] The amount to fund additional officers in schools has consistently increased after each mass shooting since 2005.[51]

During this time, there was also a proliferation across the country of zero tolerance policies in schools.[52] In the Gun Free Schools Act of 1994 signed into law by President Clinton, zero tolerance policies in schools mandated that specific punishments be imposed for carrying a firearm in schools.[53] This law was also later expanded to create mandatory suspensions or expulsions for the possession of certain drugs in school zones.[54] States, including Louisiana, also passed laws that imposed a minimum mandatory sentence for the possession of a weapon or drugs in a school zone.[55] Forty-one percent (41%) of the nation's public schools report having an SRO on campus.[56] This increase in police officer presence in schools, coupled with the proliferation of zero tolerance policies, has without question contributed to an increase in the number of children suspended or expelled from school and subsequently charged with a crime.

Ten-year-old Jaquan and twelve-year-old Javon were brothers caught fighting at a middle school. As is becoming increasingly the norm in public schools across the country, law enforcement assigned to the school were called by the classroom teacher to what was, by all accounts, simply a school fight (Did I mention that they were brothers?). By the time the incident ended, both kids were charged with battery and Javon, the oldest, was charged additionally with battery on a police officer. The officer said that he was struck by Javon, after he broke up the fight between the two brothers. Once the case finally came to court, I wanted to know the complete story. It was clear that both kids were acting out because their mother was incarcerated, and they had recently been placed in the custody of the state's child welfare system. A good counselor or social worker would have easily discovered these facts after sitting both kids down in a non-threatening setting at school. This is a perfect example of how school systems across the country have abdicated the role of disciplinarian in simple school yard fights to armed police officers, who are neither counselors nor experts in conflict resolution or child psychology.

My Dad taught 5th grade in Greenville, Mississippi, from 1956 to 1986. He had a reputation for being a stern disciplinarian in a time when teachers were allowed to mete out corporal punishment. Now, just a few months from 90 and far removed from teaching fifth graders, even he admits that he cannot imagine walking into a school with armed law enforcement officers, whose first response to a school fight is to arrest now and ask questions later.

Although the number of police officers in schools has increased exponentially in the last decade, there is no data that indicates that police in schools have improved the educational outcomes or safety of kids in school. In some cases, police officers in schools may be causing more harm by increasing the likelihood of arrest and referral to juvenile court, particularly for children of color. Students in schools deserve to learn in a safe and supportive environment, but placing law enforcement in schools with children is neither the safest nor most cost-effective method of maintaining safety in schools. A 2011 Justice Policy Institute Report found that reported incidents of violence and crime in public schools are at some of the lowest levels since the early 1990's; however, the number of arrests and referrals of students to the juvenile justice system by police officers in schools has increased exponentially.[57] Crime statistics from the Federal Bureau of Investigations from 2013 to 2018 show that over 30,000 children under the age of 10 were arrested and almost 250,000 children between the ages of 10 and 12 were arrested for the same time period.[58]

In September of 2019, a 6-year-old African American female was arrested at an Orlando, Florida, charter school by a school resource officer.[59] The officer stated that the child was having a temper tantrum and during the incident kicked an employee of the school as others tried to subdue her. The child was charged with battery and processed at the juvenile detention center. She was handcuffed, fingerprinted, and her mugshot was taken. Upon learning of the incident, the child's grandmother stated that these tantrums were the result of sleep deprivation caused by severe sleep apnea in the child, and the school was told to call her when these tantrums occurred.[60] But, even if the grandmother could not be reached, surely someone could have treated this child like their own and de-escalated the behavior without the necessity of police intervention.

Federal law requires that schools report school policing data, such as the number of children arrested by law enforcement and referred to juvenile courts. But despite this requirement, there is no national database for the collection of every arrest or referral to the juvenile justice system by police officers in schools.[61] According to the U.S. Department of Education Civil Rights Data Collection for 2015 - 2016, the most recent data available, over 290,600 cases in schools were referred to law enforcement or resulted in arrest.[62] Black students were disproportionately subject to those disciplinary measures – representing 15% of the student body and 31% of referrals, a 16% gap (up from 11% the year before).[63] Students with disabilities were also disproportionately subject to that kind of discipline, according to the data.[64]

In Louisiana, the Southern Poverty Law Center (SPLC) in its May 2019 report entitled "The Data Gap: School Policing in Louisiana," found that although schools in Louisiana are required to collect and report school policing data under the 'Every Student Succeeds Act,' schools are not accurately collecting and reporting this data.[65] The 'Every Student Succeeds' Act is a federal statute, which mandates that the Department of Education provide financial assistance to school districts under the statute's nine titles to enhance academic achievement for disadvantaged children.[66] Louisiana receives Title I funding under the Act, and thus is required to provide this data to the Department of Education.[67]

SPLC made several public records requests to Louisiana schools, but was met with incomplete and inaccurate data when compared to the Office of Civil Rights (OCR) database or that of the law enforcement agencies in question. Consequently, it is difficult to quantify whether there has been an increase in the number of young people referred to the juvenile court since the widespread implementation of SRO officers, in Louisiana, or throughout most of the country. However, anecdotally, there are many high-profile arrests of children under the age of 10, such as the 6-year-old previously discussed in this book, whose arrests have garnered national attention.

According to statistics from the Federal Bureau of Investigations from 2013 through 2018, approximately 30,000 children under the age of 10 were arrested.[68] During the same 6-year time period, 244,321 children between the ages of 10 and 12 were arrested. African American students and students with disabilities were disproportionately represented in these numbers.[69]

As a prosecutor, who worked exclusively in the juvenile justice system, well before the Columbine shootings, I have seen an exponential increase in the number of children arrested and referred to juvenile court for relatively minor offenses on school campuses, such as fighting with classmates, possessing tobacco products, or pulling a classmate's hair (yes, arrested for pulling a classmate's hair). School systems have abdicated their role as disciplinarian to campus police officers, who are not trained in child psychology or counseling or conflict resolution, but whose societal role is to enforce laws and maintain order at all costs.

I was often questioned about why I did not prosecute children arrested, who were primarily African American males, for minor offenses that arose in a school setting. In my opinion, these cases were described as minor fights between fellow classmates, outbursts in class or some other group setting, or striking a teacher or fellow student. My response was that discipline was the responsibility of the school system and not the DA or the courts. I knew that once I started prosecuting a school fight as disturbing the peace or simple battery (misdemeanors under Louisiana law, which carry a possible maximum penalty of six months in a juvenile jail), I would open a floodgate and would be inundated with cases that should have been handled at the school level with in-school or out of school suspension. But that response was not enough for some deputies, police officers, and indeed some school officials, who insisted that I prosecute such cases. I have always been a line prosecutor. This means that I am not the policymaker and my prosecutorial discretion has always been limited by the policies and directives of the elected DA. So, even if I disagreed with a directive to prosecute a school fight or vandalism at a school, my ability to refuse to comply with a directive of the elected DA was very limited, if I wanted to keep my job.

Daphne R. Robinson

5

District Attorneys Representing School Boards Is A Conflict

In the state of Louisiana, the law provides that 'the district attorneys of the several judicial districts of Louisiana, other than the parish of Orleans, shall *ex officio* be the regular attorneys and counsel for the police juries, parish school boards, and city school boards within their respective districts and of every state board or commission domiciled therein...'[70] This means that many elected district attorneys are paid by local school boards to advise and represent them, and in turn, district attorneys hire or contract with attorneys, who are considered experts in education law, to fulfill this role. This, in my opinion, creates an inherent conflict for district attorneys and further reinforces the school to prison pipeline. Because district attorneys are being paid by school boards, elected district attorneys are more inclined to respond to political pressure and do the bidding of principals and administrators, who call and request that a student be prosecuted or be given a break regardless of the circumstances.

Delinquent

In August of 2019, I was assigned the case of Charles. Charles was already on probation in the juvenile justice system when he brought a loaded gun to school and showed it off to two of his friends. He was also charged with domestic abuse battery upon his mother. Before I had the opportunity to sit down and review the case clearly, it was apparent that law enforcement and school officials wanted Charles out of school and out of school for good. He was a 16-year-old black male of imposing size with dreaded hair. I have always believed as a prosecutor in the juvenile court that it is incredibly difficult to balance public safety with doing what is in the best interest of the child. No one, not even the people that I reported to every day, wanted to see Charles as a child, who needed mental health and substance abuse treatment. But rather, everyone involved saw him as a man and a menace to be locked up as long as possible, or at least long enough to never have to go back to that school again.

When I reviewed the file, I observed the video interview of Charles and his mother conducted by the police department. At one point during the video, the police left Charles in the room alone with the video and audio playing. While alone in the room, Samuel paced back and forth talking to himself, rapping to himself, and banging his head against the wall. Unlike the police, what I saw was a very scared, troubled young man, who needed mental health and substance abuse treatment. I tried to negotiate a plea that would get Charles off the street for a while with treatment, but my discretion as an assistant district was taken away, and I was forced to prosecute every charge that Charles had in order to ensure that he would not return to public school.

Charles was eventually convicted, and his probation revoked on two charges for which he was on probation. He was sentenced by the court to an appropriate sentence in a group home. But this still was not enough for the police officers and administrators at his school. Consequently, the principal called the DA and reported that Charles had been given probation. Although this was the farthest thing from the truth, I was forced to explain why I chose to take the prosecutorial action that I had taken and was reprimanded for that decision. It was then that I realized that as a prosecutor in juvenile court making decisions, if you have no discretion, you have nothing.

6

More Mental Health Counselors Needed in Schools and Fewer Police

The case of Charles is a glaring example of one of the primary problems in schools these days – the lack of counselors, social workers, and other behavioral health workers to assist kids and their families in identifying behavioral health problems before they become debilitating. School systems have clearly chosen to use precious resources to pay for more and more police officers to patrol school hallways and corridors rather than paying for counselors and mental health providers to address unresolved mental and behavioral health issues.

National studies have found that about one in five children have a mental, emotional or behavioral disorder, but only about 20% of those children actually receive care from a mental health provider. The delay in receiving treatment often spans six to eight years for mood disorders and nine to 23 years for anxiety disorders, with longer delays for males, minorities, and lower-educated patients.[71] Adults

Daphne R. Robinson

with mental health disabilities reported the onset at around 14 years old, according to a 2005 study.[72] An increase in juvenile delinquency has been blamed in part on diagnosed and undiagnosed mental illness. The World Health Organization (WHO) predicted that psychopathology would be one the five leading causes of disability and mortality in 2020.[73]

In light of this data, what better place than schools to provide mental health services to children, because when they walk out of the school setting, there is no guarantee that families will be able to navigate the bureaucracy of the state mental health system or that they will comply with the recommendations of mental health providers. The goal is to reach kids and their families before a whole host of other problems begin to appear, such as delinquency, suicide, truancy, run away or homelessness.

One state attempting to address the mental health needs of children in the school setting is California. Mental health professionals know that once a child is diagnosed with a mental health disorder, it can be very difficult for the child and the family to attend counseling or access desperately needed prescriptions because of a lack of dependable transportation. This delay in accessing services often leads to more severe or debilitating conditions. Consequently, the California State Legislature has set aside $50 million dollars for

45

schools to develop innovative campus-based ways to detect and prevent mental illness. In 2019, the legislature passed the Mental Health Student Services Act, which incentivizes schools in the state to partner with county behavioral services in their districts to develop campus-based mental health services.[74] This program is an excellent example of meeting children and families where they are by providing school-based, mental health services in a critical domain of the socio-ecological model.

Daphne R. Robinson

7

DAs Need Data About the Children They Prosecute

One would think the broad discretion that elected District Attorneys are given by state law would encourage them to closely analyze their past transgressions, and outright neglect, of the juvenile justice system. By that I mean, we certainly know that there is overrepresentation of African American children in the juvenile justice system. Consequently, as in adult cases, we should be using data to examine whether a particular school, school zone, or zip code has an increased number of charges, what those charges are, who the kids are committing those offenses by race, age, gender, and ethnicity, who are the agencies arresting them, and why. Then we should begin asking questions about the demographics of these offenders. Do the numbers reveal that an overwhelming number of black and brown males are being arrested more than other children at a particular school in a district? What are the ages of these children? Where do they live? Do those arrested have some connection inside school and/or outside of the school? Do these arrests involve adult individuals that don't even attend the school? Who are the arresting officers? Are they arresting only black and brown males? If so, what is the articulable reason for doing so?

As prosecutors, we should not be basing our prosecutorial decision-making on outdated anecdotes and opinions from certain schools or certain parts of the community or certain school officials or certain police officers about who is a good kid and who is a bad one. As a veteran of the profession, I have heard all of the pejoratives used to justify various decisions from arrest to detention of a child, when the evidence was slight, the law was not favorable, or simply when an adult in a school decided on their own that it was time for this kid to go.

Not all DAs are bad people or racist. Sometimes the DA is the only person standing between the young person and jail, but no one knows that because the DA doesn't have the benefit of talking to the defendant. Decisions made by DAs should be based on facts, including numerical data, presented by competent individuals who understand the integration and evaluation of data in the criminal justice system.

In 2005, the Rapides District Attorney's Office was chosen as a Models for Change Juvenile Justice Reform site. The initiative was created and funded by the MacArthur Foundation. Our jurisdiction was chosen as one of several prosecutor's offices across the country to create alternatives to the formal processing and detention of kids in the court system. This initiative began with overhauling the office's outdated computer system used to collect juvenile data. In 2005, not only was the system used to collect juvenile data outdated and obsolete, no one in the District Attorney's office had an email address or access to email at the time. That process taught us a great deal about collecting, analyzing, and evaluating data. I learned that when it comes to data, everyone in the juvenile justice system needs it, but very few individuals in the system have access to it or understand the power of having it. I learned that without adequate data it is impossible for judges, prosecutors, probation officers, and service providers to make decisions that yield the best possible outcomes for public safety and for the youth and families that we serve, while also being efficient with time and resources. Juvenile justice systems across the country are turning to evidence-based policies and performance measures to help them to better understand their court system, develop research-driven reforms, and evaluate outcomes. To do this, good, reliable data is essential.

In a report by the ACLU called 'Unlocking the Black Box: How the Prosecutorial Transparency Act Will Empower Communities and Help End Mass Incarceration,' Nicole Zaya Fortier writes, "In most cities and counties, elected prosecutors report very little public data on critical decisions–for example, how they make charging decisions and who is given a second chance, and why. Prosecutors seldom even make public the policies that guide the powers they exercise on a daily basis. Using open records laws to obtain information from prosecutors' offices is often difficult and time-consuming. While a growing number of prosecutors' offices have started making some information public, these efforts are piecemeal and subject to change depending on who's in office."[75]

This statement is doubly true when it comes to critical data in juvenile cases. It has been my experience that juvenile data in DA's offices in Louisiana is collected by one person, such as an office administrator or administrative secretary, with inadequate systems that do not communicate well with other systems. Data is usually only collected for the purpose of state and federal funding, state and federal statistical inquiries, such as demographics, or for the purpose of justifying private or public grant resources. Most offices do not even collect the most basic data about juvenile cases nor have they invested in the necessary infrastructure to access and evaluate this data. This problem does not just exist in DA's offices across Louisiana, but it also exists in DA's offices across the United States.[76]

The most comprehensive nationwide survey of state prosecutors' offices, completed by the Urban Institute in 2018, found limited prosecutorial data collection even for basic case information.[77] The survey focused in part on "foundational case information," including the volume of cases coming into an office, the number of charges, and what happens within a case. Results revealed that less than half of the offices interviewed collect all of these basic data points. Even fewer publish the results – only 24 percent reported making their data analyses public.[78]

This lack of data collection and transparency have long been the norm among prosecutors' offices for a variety of reasons. First, there are almost no legal requirements that they collect data.[79] Laws rarely mandate the recording or public disclosure of substantive prosecutorial data, nor do they require prosecutors' offices to make their policies public. Next, prosecutors' offices have been particularly slow, when compared with other law enforcement actors, like police departments and correctional facilities, to accept the need for data collection and to create systems to capture it.[80] In addition, citizens demanding change in the criminal legal system have largely focused on the lack of transparency from police, and only recently have turned their attention to prosecutors. In other words, prosecutors have not been subject to much external pressure or political consequences for operating their offices as "black boxes."[81]

8

What happened to this kid?

While preparing for a presentation about Adverse Childhood Experiences at Louisiana State University in Shreveport, Louisiana, I heard the rapper Meek Mill on the podcast "Song Exploder" explain the origins of the lyrics of his song "Trauma," from the album *Championships*. It is said to be some of the best song-writing of his career. In it, Mill describes his early days as a rapper in North Philadelphia and his several months-long detention in a Pennsylvania prison for probation violation. After an appeal of his case, his original conviction was eventually overturned by the Pennsylvania Supreme Court in 2019.

This song summed up in a few minutes what it took me years to realize. Sometimes those of us working in the system have absolutely no idea what has happened in the lives of some of these kids. Fathers are incarcerated. Mothers are addicted to cocaine or opioids. And the kids are being raised by grandmothers, aunts, and other surrogates. Many times, these children have been physically, sexually, and emotionally abused by people inside and outside of their household. They have witnessed their mothers physically abused by fathers, boyfriends, and strangers. Exposure to gun violence is sometimes a common part of life. Are they angry? Of course! And they have every right to be!

After I graduated from public health school and eventually returned to my work as a prosecutor in the juvenile justice system, I told myself that I would stop asking, 'What's wrong with this kid?' and I would start asking, 'What happened to this kid?' This kind of stress – the kind of stress described in "Trauma" – can become toxic when the events or conditions precipitating it are severely frightening or threatening—especially when they are sustained or frequently repeated—and when protective factors are insufficient to mitigate the stress to tolerable levels. Then, toxic stress can produce not only heightened focus but the opposite result, a decrease in performance levels.[82] When frightening or threatening situations occur too frequently, stress becomes chronic and disrupts the brain's and body's responses. The body can over or underproduce necessary hormones, and the body's physiology can fail to return to normal. This is a toxic stress response.[83] Until I began to understand and recognize adverse childhood experiences, otherwise known as ACEs, or toxic stress in children, I did not appreciate why so many of the kids in the juvenile justice system were so angry, so sad, and so broken.

The Adverse Childhood Experiences (ACEs) Study was conducted at Kaiser Permanente California in conjunction with Dr. Robert Anda of the Centers for Disease Control (CDC) from 1995 to 1997.[84] The prospective study included 17,421 insured, well educated, adult patients, who received physical examinations and completed confidential surveys regarding childhood experiences and their current health status and behaviors.[85] The Family Health History and Health Appraisal Questionnaire were used to collect information on child abuse and neglect, household challenges and other socio-behavioral factors in the ACEs Study. The questions refer to the first 18 years of life for the respondent. All of the questions about adverse childhood experiences are categorized into three groups: abuse, neglect, and household challenges.

From the study, it was learned that there are 10 adverse child experiences that contribute to negative health and life outcomes.[86] They include:

Abuse:

☐ **Emotional abuse:** A parent, stepparent, or adult living in your home swore at you, insulted you, put you down, or acted in a way that made you afraid that you might be physically hurt.

☐ **Physical abuse:** A parent, stepparent, or adult living in your home pushed, grabbed, slapped, threw something at you, or hit you so hard that you had marks or were injured.

☐ **Sexual abuse:** An adult, relative, family friend, or stranger who was at least 5 years older than you touched or fondled your body in a sexual way, made you touch his/her body in a sexual way, attempted to have any type of sexual intercourse with you.

Household Challenges:

☐ **Mother treated violently:** Your mother or stepmother was pushed, grabbed, slapped, had something thrown at her,was kicked, bitten, hit with a fist, hit with something hard, repeatedly hit for over at least a few minutes, or ever threatened or hurt by a knife or gun by your father (or stepfather) or mother's boyfriend.

☐ **Substance abuse in the household:** A household member was a problem drinker or alcoholic or a household member used street drugs.

☐ **Mental illness in the household:** A household member was depressed or mentally ill or a household member attempted suicide.

☐ **Parental separation or divorce:** Your parents were ever separated or divorced.

☐ **Incarcerated household member:** A household member went to prison.

Neglect:

☐ **Emotional and physical neglect:** A household member fails to meet a child's basic emotional and physical needs. These needs include housing, food, clothing, education, and access to medical care.[87]

The major findings of the study tell us that ACEs are across all populations. Almost one-third of the participants in the study had at least one ACE, and more than one in five participants reported three or more ACEs.[88] Some populations are more vulnerable to experiencing ACEs, like juvenile justice-involved youth, because of the social and economic conditions in which they live, learn, work, and play.

The ACE score is the total sum of the different categories of ACEs reported by the participants. As the number of ACEs increase so does the risk for negative outcomes. Some of these negative health and life outcomes include:

- Alcoholism and alcohol abuse
- Chronic Obstructive pulmonary disease (COPD)
- Depression
- Fetal Death
- Decreased quality of life because of health
- Illicit drug use
- Ischemic Heart Disease
- Liver Disease
- Risk for Intimate Partner Violence
- Multiple Sexual Partners
- Sexually Transmitted Diseases
- Smoking
- Suicide Attempts
- Unintended Pregnancies
- Early initiation of sexual activity

⬚ Adolescent pregnancy.

Children involved in the juvenile justice system and in the child welfare system often have higher ACE scores, which often includes having an incarcerated parent in childhood.[89] A higher ACE score puts many of these children at greatest risk to continue to reoffend at an even more violent level.[90] As a result of the prolonged exposure to toxic stress, neurological and psychological changes occur making the maltreated child more prone to violence. The consequences of this can include anxiety, impaired memory, and mood control. Criminological and public health research suggest that childhood trauma and adversity are the most significant risk factors for predicting future criminal conduct.[91]

I have spent most of my professional career in juvenile court as a prosecutor listening to traumatic life stories from children aged 10 to 18 years that have literally made me cry in open court. But it has taken far too long for those of us in the juvenile court system to recognize the impact of traumatic experiences on children and their behavior. In the early days of my career as a prosecutor, I thought my only responsibility was to prosecute the child for the delinquent act committed and others (judges, probation officers, counselors) would take care of the rest. But, when I started to see the same kids return to juvenile court with the same or worse behavior, I knew that once a kid walked out of the courtroom, there was no guarantee that services were being provided that actually addressed the root causes of the trauma contributing to the behavior. After years of asking questions and demanding appropriate services for kids (when it really wasn't my responsibility to demand), I have decided that these services must be mandated by public policy and applied across the board to all children that enter the juvenile court.

In the words of Kristen B. Schubert, a former health policy analyst at the Centers for Disease Control who now directs the Vulnerable Populations Program at the Robert Wood Johnson Foundation, "This new knowledge [about ACEs] calls for a population-based public health approach much like what was done for smoking, seatbelts, and drunk driving." For example, in the book *Law in Public Health Practice*, mandatory seat-belt laws, their enforcement, and appropriate public awareness campaigns have been shown to be very effective in increasing rates of seat-belt wearing and thus, decreasing the number of motor-vehicle related fatalities.[92] Law-based interventions at the federal level in 1968 required all new cars sold in the United States to be equipped with seat belts, and later mandatory requirements followed for headrests, air bags, and other mandatory built-in safety features.[93] Congress also combined funding incentives and penalties to encourage states to enact and enforce seat-belt laws. Focusing on driver behavior as a risk factor, state governments later followed suit and imposed speed limits and other restrictions on driving. Seat belt laws, and all the other legal restrictions on motor vehicle operations, have contributed to the reduction of motor-vehicle related deaths and morbidity in the latter part of the 21st century.[94]

By definition, juvenile offenders are a vulnerable population who should not be stigmatized or cast aside as broken or defective, but should be considered political and legal subjects, who deserve the full attention and protection of the state through law and policy. This attention and protection should include educating communities, schools, and juvenile courts about the early identification of ACEs with the goal of improving the general health and reducing future medical, social services, and criminal justice costs for these vulnerable youth.

When school personnel, health professionals or juvenile justice professionals observe behaviors such as substance abuse, overeating, disruptive classroom behavior, and bullying, a screening for a history of ACEs should be obtained and used to determine the appropriate intervention. Immediately suspending or expelling or arresting a child when such behaviors are exhibited may deprive children of the only safe place that they have to go. Addressing the harmful effects of ACEs on this vulnerable population will require legal and state supported interventions and public awareness campaigns to increase the level of knowledge about ACEs-related morbidity and mortality, particularly in the juvenile justice system.

The socio-ecological model in public health helped me to understand that in order to do what's in the best interest of a child, the system participants cannot just focus on the individual behavior of a juvenile, but they must also appreciate how current conditions, such as toxic stress, within the primary domains of the child's family, school, and community can contribute to their success or their delinquency. These conditions within the primary domains are called social determinants of health and include poverty, unequal access to health care, poor environmental conditions and educational inequities, race/ethnicity, employment, sexual orientation, and geographic location, as well as the structures and systems that shape the daily conditions of life.[95] Health, in this context, is interpreted broadly to not just include physical health, but those factors that make children healthy, mentally stable, and productive people.

Kathy came into the juvenile justice system because her family failed her. She was charged with status offenses, running away from home and skipping school. These are offenses that are only considered crimes when committed by a juvenile in certain states. At the hearing to determine whether Kathy would be placed in a group home for girls, the court learned that Kathy's adopted mother was really not the legally adoptive parent. Apparently, she and her lawyer had failed to complete the necessary paperwork to finalize the adoption. Once the putative adoptive mother, who happened to be white, learned that she no longer legally had responsibility for Kathy, she told the court that she no longer wanted custody of the child. Kathy knew who her biological father was and had been in contact with him off and on over the years. She wanted the court to give her a chance to live with him. The father, who was African-American, testified that he had a brief relationship with Kathy's biological mother when he was in the military. He blamed the biological mother for keeping him away from Kathy and told the court that she could come to live with him. After hearing the heartbreaking testimony of both Kathy and her father, everyone, including me, wanted so desperately for this to work. Kathy was placed on probation and sent back to detention until such time that her father could make arrangements for her to come live with him in Texas. After weeks of lying to Kathy and her probation officer, it became clear that her father was not willing to make the sacrifices necessary to provide for the child. Kathy was placed in a group home, where she was eventually stalked by a human trafficker who offered her the love and security that she desperately wanted from her father. She was eventually kidnapped by her trafficker and taken to Dallas, Texas for several weeks and forced into the sex trade. Fortunately, one day while riding with her trafficker in Dallas, the car was pulled over by police and the trafficker was arrested for being a felon in possession of a handgun. Kathy was returned to the jurisdiction and placed in the dual custody of juvenile justice and child welfare because she had nowhere to go.

The family is one of the most important domains in the socio-ecological model. Family is one of the single most important influences in a child's life.[96] From their first moments of life, children depend on parents and family to protect them and provide for their needs. Parents and family form a child's first relationships. They are a child's first teachers and act as role models in how to act and how to experience the world around them. Families who are engaged in the life of the child provide a protective barrier against the kind of behavior exhibited by Kathy. However, when parents, guardians, and other family members are dealing with their own problems such as homelessness, substance abuse, unemployment or incarceration, it is difficult for them to provide the kind of support that is so desperately needed by children.

Daphne R. Robinson

9

The Foster Care to Prison Pipeline for Children of Color

As juvenile justice advocates, we have done a good job of educating the public about the "school to prison pipeline" – the disturbing national trend where children are funneled out of schools into the juvenile and criminal justice systems through zero tolerance policies and the over policing of schools. However, we have done a poor job of educating the public about the child welfare system and the adverse impact it has on children of color and their families.

In my years as a prosecutor, I have seen children victimized by parents, guardians, and caretakers in just about every way imaginable. The pictures of children as young as three or four years old burned with curling irons or beaten with extension cords or living in meth-house squalor will be forever etched in my mind. These are the kinds of cases that make even the most jaded, hardcore homicide prosecutors weep. Prosecuting the parents of abused or neglected children was some of the hardest work that I did as a prosecutor – not because of the parents but because of the children. It is work that still haunts me to this day. And it is another area of the juvenile justice system in which children of color are overrepresented, even though research shows these racial disparities are not due to higher incidences of abuse and neglect in black families as compared to white families.[97] In reality, these racial disparities exist in the child welfare system for many of the same reasons that they exist in the juvenile justice system – institutional and systemic racism. Sadly, because the child welfare system, particularly foster care, has become a feeder for the juvenile justice system, the child welfare system serves as yet another pipeline into the juvenile justice system for black children.

Studies show that about one in ten black children – more than twice the rate of white children – experience foster care placement.[98] And, once those children are removed from their homes and placed into foster care, studies show further that they are more likely than other children in the general population to experience incarceration in the juvenile justice system.[99] Additionally, incarcerated adults are disproportionately more likely to have been in foster care, reinforcing the "foster-care-to-prison-pipeline" for children of color.[100]

Once children of color are identified by juvenile justice professionals as dual status youth – stuck in both the juvenile justice system and the child welfare system – these children are more likely to move deeper into the juvenile justice system, which includes detention, probation or subsequent juvenile incarceration. Research suggests that dual status youth often do more than simply "touch" the juvenile justice system. A study conducted in Illinois revealed that foster youth are more likely to experience formal processing in the juvenile justice system, which can lead to deeper involvement. Notably, the Illinois study concludes that: "Since youths coming to the juvenile justice system from child welfare are disproportionately likely to be African-American, this bias in decision-making contributes to disproportionate minority contact." Ultimately, deeper system penetration results in increased individual and system costs and worse outcomes for youth.[101]

As someone who has done this work for a very long time, I know that when court professionals, including prosecutors and judges, realize that a child has had contact with child welfare, there is a tendency to believe that we must demand more from the child in order to protect them. Sometimes that means more supervision or more probation, when child welfare may be better able to address the delinquent behavior with more behavioral counseling or mental health treatment. This requires that court personnel and probation officers in juvenile court work closely with caseworkers and case managers in child welfare to create a case plan that is coordinated and addresses the whole child's needs.

A study from Los Angeles County revealed that almost two-thirds of youth who were involved in both the child welfare and juvenile probation systems had a stay in an adult jail within four years of exiting from juvenile systems. Additionally, the study found that dual status youth were far more likely to be heavy users of public systems, less likely to have high educational attainment, and less likely to be consistently employed.[102] Thus, it would seem reasonable that if the number of children going into foster care was reduced, the number of children of color ending up in the juvenile justice system and the adult criminal justice system would be reduced as well.[103]

This data confirms what I have known anecdotally for years while working in the juvenile court. When I first started working at the DA's office in 1996, I attended our morning staff meetings. The purpose was for the prosecutors who handled adult felony cases to discuss which cases would be tried the following week and usually little else. When a case was mentioned, sometimes I tried to explain that I had prosecuted the same defendant's parents for abuse and neglect when the defendant was a child. Later, I prosecuted the same defendant, who was usually an African-American male, when he was a child for missing school or running away. This usually led to more serious delinquency charges when the child grew older. I often wondered aloud what had the system done to fail this child who was now an adult being tried for armed robbery, rape or murder. When I realized no one in those meetings ever seemed to care about the connection between child neglect and abuse, truancy, delinquency, and adult criminal behavior, I stopped attending the meetings, and began to use my time identifying ways to break the cycle for the next generation of black youth in the system.

10

Where is your parent?

Michelle Alexander in her book *The New Jim Crow*, implored those of us who consider ourselves criminal justice advocates to grab the baton and run the race that she started in this field. She said, "This book focuses on the experience of African American men in the new caste system [the phenomenon of mass incarceration and its implications for racial justice]. I hope other scholars and advocates will pick up where the book leaves off and develop the critique more fully or apply the themes sketched here to other groups and other contexts."[104] This book is my effort to pick up the mantle and develop the thesis that the juvenile justice system has failed black youth. However, it is difficult to tell the story of black children in the juvenile justice system without 'plowing tilled ground' by discussing mass incarceration and its impact on black communities and the children that live in them.

From a public health perspective, community is another level of the socio-ecological model. It represents one more level of influence that shapes the lives of African American children. The socio-ecological model assumes that not only do these levels act independently in shaping behavior, they are also interactive.[105] The most success in affecting behavior is achieved when all of the levels of the model are engaged simultaneously. Thus, improving schools, implementing child welfare reform, and providing parents with the resources and support that they need in their communities can have a transformative effect on the lives of black children, and will serve as protective factors from delinquent behavior.

Protective factors are those factors that modify, ameliorate or alter a child's response to environmental risk that predisposes him or her to maladaptive behavior.[106] For instance, if a child is in foster care but lives in a supportive community and attends a well-funded school with engaged teachers who understand how to balance discipline and public safety, the negative effects of living in a foster home will hopefully be ameliorated. However, if a child lives with their grandmother in a neighborhood which has been decimated by mass incarceration, in which adult fathers, brothers, and uncles are behind bars, that experience of parental imprisonment can have long lasting negative effects on children.

The sociologist David Garland first used a variant of the term mass incarceration and defined it as "historically and comparatively extreme levels of incarceration that are so heavily concentrated among groups that incarceration has become a normal stage in the life course."[107] The resultant effects of mass incarceration on children in the juvenile justice system have become normalized as well. One of those norms is the number of children, currently in the juvenile justice system, who have or have had, one or both parents incarcerated. The phenomenon is so common in my experience as a prosecutor, it is no longer strange or unusual.

Kevin and Quan were living with their mother at the time the boys were sexually assaulted by their mother's boyfriend. By the time I met the boys, their biological father had just been released from prison and the children had been placed in the home of their paternal grandmother by child welfare. The boys were living in the home with their grandmother and their father. The boys clearly loved their father, but I wondered how he would be able to navigate life as a convicted felon with no job and no place of his own in which to live with his kids. How long would it take before he decided to give up trying to prove that he was rehabilitated and had paid his debt to society?

The United States has the highest rate of adult incarceration in the world, and that rate of incarceration disproportionately affects black and Latino populations in this country. In 2018, there were 2.3 million people in state and federal prisons across the U.S.[108] In 2017, there were 1,549 black prisoners for every 100,000 black adults -- nearly six times the imprisonment rate for whites (272 per 100,000).[109]

Before this period of mass incarceration, which spans from the 1970s to today, it was rare to have a family member incarcerated, particularly a parent. However, roughly 8% of children in the United States born in 1990 had a father imprisoned by the age of 14.[110] Today, having a family member imprisoned is disproportionately higher for African American children than for white children. Sadly, 25% of African American children have a parent who is imprisoned at some point in their childhood, as compared to white children, who only have a 3% chance of having a parent incarcerated at some point during their childhood.[111] Although maternal imprisonment is less common than paternal imprisonment, it occurs more frequently among African American children than white children.[112]

These numbers are staggering and contribute to the destabilization of African American families and communities where children of color live. When an adult male, who is a father, is incarcerated, research shows that his health and earning potential is diminished. It also increases the risk of divorce and separation and affects the financial well-being of wives and girlfriends that are left behind.[113] Another consequence of mass incarceration is that the majority of black women are unmarried today, including 70 percent of professional black women.[114] And as Michelle Alexander points out in her book *The New Jim Crow*, "because the drug war has been raging for decades now, the parents of children coming of age today were targets of the drug war as well. As a result, many fathers are in prison, and those who are "free" bear the prison label. They are often unable to provide for, or meaningfully contribute to, a family. Any wonder, then, that many youth embrace their stigmatized identity as a means of survival in this new caste system?"[115] Most notably for those of us who work in the juvenile justice system, the incarceration of adult males, who are fathers, leads to aggression, behavioral problems, and social marginalization of their children.

In a recent article in the *Atlantic Magazine* entitled "How Incarceration Infects a Community," Emily Von Hoffman explores the collateral damage to communities and families caused by mass incarceration. In it, she cites several prominent public health researchers who have concluded that incarceration should be treated as a contagion because the closer the proximity to the person incarcerated (or infected) the greater the risk of that person becoming incarcerated.[116] She cites the book ***A Plague of Prisons: The Epidemiology of Mass Incarceration*** by Ernest Drucker, which points out that young minority men are the most susceptible to the contagion of incarceration, poor urban neighborhoods are the hardest hit, and the children growing up in affected families are the most likely to have shortened life expectancies and are six to seven times more likely to become infected (incarcerated) than children in unaffected families.[117] Of particular concern is the effect of constant surveillance of the formerly incarcerated and their families on the mental health of children.[118] The most profound effects of incarceration on the health of a community are that former prisoners and their families often remain locked in low socioeconomic status, unemployment, and unstable housing.[119] Having an incarcerated parent is also considered one of the most significant adverse childhood experiences and may lock the child in a continuous feed loop of poverty, poor health, and poor life outcomes.

11

Safe Communities Build Resilience

In my years of prosecuting delinquency and abuse cases, I have seen children who have endured some unbelievably cruel and traumatic experiences. I have always wondered why some children survive those experiences and go on to live healthy, productive lives, while others get caught up in a cycle of negative life outcomes that may lead them to adult incarceration or early death. Why are some children, who have experienced these traumatic events, more resilient than others? Resilience is the ability to adapt successfully in the face of significant stress, adversity or trauma.[120] Protective factors are those factors which buffer the effects of stressful and traumatic experiences.[121] The presence or absence of these factors must exist at each level of the socioecological model before, during, and after traumatic events.

At the interpersonal or relationship level, there must be a strong, caring primary caregiver and reliable mentors in the child's life. One of the programs that I have personally seen effectively serve low-income, marginalized families is the Nurse Family Partnership (NFP). The Nurse Family Partnership is an evidence-based program for low-income (those making under $9.000), first time mothers that sends nurses into the homes of women, often single, and teenagers with only a high school education who are pregnant for the first time.[122] The nurses are professional registered nurses with at least a Bachelor of Science degree in nursing. These nurses continue to visit the home until the child is two years of age, covering things such as diet, breast-feeding, safety, parenting skills, age-appropriate toys, and mental health.[123]

According to a study by James J. Heckman, a Nobel laureate economist at the University of Chicago, "Children, who receive home visits are healthier, achieve more in school, and have better social and emotional skills."[124] What is even more exciting for juvenile justice professionals is that NFP has been shown to have a particularly strong and lasting effect on boys, which confirms existing research that has found that boys are more vulnerable to poverty and disadvantage, while girls tend to be more resilient.[125] Dr. Heckman said in a July 2017 article in the New York Times about the program, "There is a boy problem in this country, especially for disadvantaged boys, and working with the mothers changing their environment seems to have an effect on their [boys'] well-being."[126]

Policymakers and skeptics of the program will often argue that NFP costs too much because it utilizes professionally trained nurses, who make regular home visits for two and a half years. It is estimated that the operating budget for NFP services provided to 100 participants would cost approximately $450,000 to 500,000 annually, depending on the local salaries for registered nurses. However, given the measurable outcomes of the program, the cost of $4,500 per family is quite low when compared to the cost savings associated with a reduction in emergency and hospital services, public welfare, social services, juvenile justice, and adult corrections. As a matter of fact, economic analyses indicate that when it serves low-income, first-time teenage mothers, NFP pays for itself by the time the children of those mothers reach the age of 4.[127]

Next, schools and communities should offer safe, place-based environments that reduce stressors for poor children of color and enhance their perception of feeling safe in their own communities and schools. This has been shown to fill the void in adolescents' lives, which results from living in extremely stressed families and communities characterized by poverty, high crimes rates, and a lack of opportunity. Community-based programs offer the opportunity for young people to develop supportive relationships with adults, a sense of belonging and membership, and the opportunity to develop healthy adolescent behaviors. Programs with these qualities have been found to be an integral, contributing factor to the development of resilience and positive self-identity.[128] One of the worst feelings as a prosecutor is to see a kid released from probation or custody after participating in a great program that has markedly changed their personality and behavior, and then realize that he will return to the same community that he came from with no family or community-based support. I believe juvenile courts have a responsibility to ensure that young people return to communities in which they have a chance to succeed. Some people will say that courts have no control over the community to which the child returns. I completely disagree and have seen wise judges return children to an alternate guardian or relative placement because the community is more supportive and has community-based programs that include neighborhood residents and volunteers, and provide services that are not readily available in the neighborhood in which the child typically lives. Some of these services include job training, group counseling, life-skills training, family counseling and substance abuse education. These kinds of programs are also considered protective because they prevent further penetration in the juvenile justice system or prevent transition into the adult criminal system.

One of the community-based programs that fits this criteria is the YouthBuild Program. YouthBuild is a comprehensive program targeting low-income young adults, who have troubled pasts.[129] The program is a targeted intervention that focuses on 16 to 24-year old low-income offenders.

The program includes 'a combination of education, skill-building, counseling, leadership development, community service, positive values and relationships, high standards of behavior, and clear pathways to a productive future.'[130] The program is a national nonprofit founded in 1990. It is described as a 9-month to 12-month long program in which youth spend half their time learning construction trade skills by building or rehabilitating housing for low-income people. The other half of the time is spent in a YouthBuild classroom earning a high school diploma or equivalency degree. Counseling, life skills training, and financial management are also taught.[131]

In a study published in the publication **_Youth Violence and Juvenile Justice_** in 2010, researchers concluded that several key findings emerged from the analysis of the YouthBuild.[132] First, the YB graduates were more likely to graduate from high school or obtain a GED when compared to dropouts from the program. Second, overall, YB graduates had lower rates of offending than those who dropped out of the program. Finally, a subsequent study of older YB graduates finds significant evidence of a long-term positive outcome for many participants.[133] Programs like YouthBuild serve as significant protective institutions in the community because they promote adolescent development and prevent further penetration into the child welfare, juvenile justice, and criminal justice systems.[134]

Another community-based program for children is called Project Spirit. Project Spirit is a Saint-Paul, Minnesota based, at-risk after school program designed to help students get the nutritious meal that they need in a safe, supervised

Daphne R. Robinson

environment. The program is funded by the St. Paul
Area Council of Churches and also provides
academic enrichment activities and strengthens
children's identity as people of African descent.[135]

The program helps to build resilience by
providing a safe place where students feel valued.
Students engage with culturally appropriate learning
models, which help to build a strong sense of
identity and heritage. The curriculum is organized
around seven principles of African culture and uses
traditional African tools, such as call-and-response
activities and songs to recognize and congratulate
each other for success.[136] The staff is primarily
African American. Community programs such as
Project Spirit are successful because they build
resilience by using cultural support to guard against
negative risk factors for delinquency.[137]

Some may ask why Project Spirit focuses on
the culture of people of African descent. From my
perspective as a prosecutor, who happens to be an
African-American female, I understand the value of
providing children of color with information about
their own culture, society, and their role in society
with programming that is culturally competent. The
significance of what it means to be black in twenty-
first century America is critical, in my opinion, to
the well-being of African American children.
Studies show that racial identity has been
determined to be a protective factor for African
American males and moderates the risk of violent
behavior in certain circumstances.[138]

12

Policy Recommendations to Reduce the Number of African-American Children in the Juvenile Justice System and to Improve the Juvenile Justice Systems Response (Takeaways)

If you have made it to the last chapter of the book, you know by now that the juvenile justice system itself can be detrimental to African American youth, who start with historical disadvantages that have been outlined in the preceding chapters. My suggestions to repair the system, which follow, are not novel. On the contrary, they are practical, common sense approaches that have been applied in other jurisdictions. So, I'm sure you're asking yourself what's the problem? Why can't the juvenile justice system and all the players in it, get its act together and apply these approaches? Well, the juvenile justice **system** is just that – **a system**. And system reform is incredibly difficult. However, I contend that it can be done, but it will take the collective voices and cries of probation officers, judges, prosecutors, public defenders, advocates, families, and policymakers to make it happen.

Recommendation #1: Defund the Police

I began writing this book while hospitalized after a major car accident in 2019. Once I returned home and began moving towards a normal life again, a global pandemic ensued. As of this writing, there are over 2,000,000 people who have tested positive for COVID-19, a respiratory virus, in the United States. Nationwide, over 119,000 deaths have resulted from the spread of the virus. Tragically, African Americans continue to experience the highest overall mortality rate from the disease in the country. Just when I thought it couldn't get any worse, the country collectively witnessed the death of George Floyd, an unarmed, non-resisting black man, accused of passing a twenty-dollar counterfeit bill, as a former Minneapolis police officer placed his knee on his neck for 8 minutes and 46 seconds. This sadistic act of police brutality sparked protests all over the country, which have led to the high pitched cries from activists urging elected officials to **'defund the police'** across the country. This phrase has come to mean completely rethinking the priorities of the criminal justice system and how we fund those priorities. To criminal justice reform activists, this means reallocating the millions of dollars presently poured into police departments by state and federal governments back into marginalized communities of color to support people and provide services.

I agree with rethinking and reallocating funding for police departments, and propose that funds presently used by police and sheriff departments to place armed police officers in school settings be reallocated to public health departments to provide mental health services and counseling in schools. Immediately after the calls to 'defund the police' began in the wake of the death of George Floyd, members of the Prince Georges County, Maryland School Board recommended divesting funding currently used to fund armed police officers in schools to add more mental health professionals, counselors, and elementary school reading interventionists. Not only would such a proposal save the community money and be a useful reallocation of funding, it would also be a gigantic step towards dismantling the school to prison pipeline. David Murray, a member of the school board in Prince George's County, said in June of 2020, "What we're saying is that there's not a place for police officers, armed police officers in Prince George's County Public Schools and only that … we think that the money can be better served supporting our students with more social workers, more mental health professionals, more academic interventionists to get elementary school students reading on grade level."[139]

Recommendation #2: Create a national database of juvenile arrest data

All police agencies and district attorney's offices that receive public funding should be mandated to collect, analyze, and report data about

Daphne R. Robinson

juvenile arrests and juvenile court referrals to a national database. The number of children referred to juvenile court, the location of the alleged crime, and the demographics of the offender should be just some of the data that is collected. Once collected, the data should be disaggregated by race, gender, age, and any other necessary demographic, to determine which agencies arrest a disproportionate number of minority children and why. Additionally, this data should then be made available for public comment and review. This information will allow policymakers to track in real time the number of juveniles arrested and prosecuted using concrete data rather than just anecdotal evidence.

Recommendation #3: Prohibit Conflicts of Interest

District Attorney's Offices with jurisdiction over juvenile offenders should be prohibited from representing school boards in the same jurisdiction to avoid the appearance of impropriety, and to prevent school officials from attempting to exercise undue influence over the prosecution or dismissal of juvenile cases. And much like the calls for 'defunding the police,' funds previously paid to DA's office for legal services should be redirected to school-centered, evidence-based restorative justice programs, such as Restorative Circle. Restorative Circle is a conflict-resolution dialogue circle, in which those affected develop their own solutions about how to address the problem. In this process, a facilitator trained by the Center for Restorative Approaches brings together students responsible for the conflict in the school setting, de-escalates tensions, and assists the parties in creating an action plan to repair harm and prevent it from happening again. The Center for Restorative Approaches is based in New Orleans and its mission is to 'provide schools, workplaces, and other communities with training, consulting, and facilitation of dialogue circles which improve communication, build relationships, reduce violence, and allow those most impacted by conflict and wrongdoing to develop their own solutions for justice and well-being.'[140]

Recommendation #4: Implicit Bias Training

Ongoing implicit bias training should be mandated for all juvenile court personnel. Implicit or unconscious bias occurs when people make decisions based partly on stereotypes without being aware that the stereotype has influenced them. In one example of implicit bias, studies show that adult participants perceive black children as older and less innocent than white children in the same age group.[141] Although implicit bias is pervasive, it is also malleable, making it possible to unlearn many of our internal biases.[142] As discussed throughout this book, the origin of the juvenile court system is mired in institutional and systemic racism. And although there are many people of goodwill of all races and ethnicities working throughout juvenile courts, implicit bias training is still necessary to teach these people of goodwill how to avoid making decisions based on the race or socio-economic background of a young person rather than the specifics of the case. When implicit bias training is offered to juvenile court personnel, it is frequently offered on a short-term or a one-time event basis, if offered at all. Such limited training is insufficient to address the difficult issues of race or class bias. Consequently, the training should be incorporated into the continuing education requirements that court personnel must acquire as a part of their individual disciplines.

Recommendation #5: Trauma-informed Training

Just like implicit bias training, trauma-informed training should also be mandated for all court personnel and those who influence the outcomes of justice-involved youth. Since children of color in the juvenile justice system are more likely to have at least one parent incarcerated, more likely to have been a witness to or victim of gun violence or more likely to have been the victim of a sexual assault, it is imperative that court personnel be trained to recognize the signs and symptoms of trauma, be able to assess it, and recommend culturally, competent trauma-focused therapy and counseling. Every child that is at risk of being removed from their home for delinquent behaviors should be assessed by the court for trauma and adverse childhood experiences or ACEs. And if trauma or an elevated ACE score is confirmed, the child and their guardian should be required to participate in community and evidence-based, trauma-focused therapy as a part of any sentence or disposition provided by a culturally competent provider.

Delinquent

It is imperative for policymakers to acknowledge that justice-involved youth have higher rates of trauma, and that the trauma begins earlier in life and persists over time. Because research shows that the brain continues to develop into early adulthood, the juvenile justice system has a role in helping many of these children heal from the trauma that they have suffered. Whenever a child interacts with the court system – whether it is family court, child protection, or juvenile delinquency – the system should endeavor to mitigate the harm already done and do no further harm to the child.[143] Moreover, attorneys that represent children, and those that prosecute cases in juvenile court, should be aware that traumatic stress may interfere with the way that a child interacts with an attorney. The child, already in a vulnerable position, may be even more reluctant to reveal critical information that could be outcome determinative. Past traumatic experiences may prevent the child from forming a relationship of trust with an attorney or other juvenile justice professionals.[144] Policies and practices that support a trauma-informed juvenile justice system should mandate trauma screening and assessment, using the ACE Calculator or other validated screening instrument; evidence-based trauma treatment; and cross-system engagement to promote resilience and engagement among youth and families.[145]

Recommendation #6: Reallocate Juvenile Justice Funding Towards a Public Health Approach

Daphne R. Robinson

Amid the cries of activists to defund the police, there are many who have also suggested the same for juvenile courts. Proponents of this proposal point to the fact that juvenile crime has steadily decreased from 2008 to 2018, while the presence of police in schools has increased 100 fold over the same period of time. This increase in police presence has escalated the severity of responses to behaviors, many of which would previously have been handled by school personnel. Money allocated to juvenile courts by state, local and federal governments could be reallocated to community-based treatment and services for children and their families.

When I began writing this book, I didn't have a crystal ball. I never dreamed that as I began writing the last sections of this book that as a country, we would be reeling from the effects of two pandemics – COVID-19 and institutional racism. The events of the first half of the year have put into sharp focus that many of the problems of this country emanate from systemic racism embedded into the fabric of every state funded and state sanctioned system in this country. As a veteran of the juvenile justice system, I have been frustrated and angry about what we do wrong, but I never thought I'd arrive at this point. However, in light of everything I have read and written, I have decided that I completely concur with the arguments raised by those who advocate defunding the juvenile justice system dollar by dollar.

Why? Here are my three simple truths.

1. The current state of the juvenile justice system is failing black kids.
2. The current state of the juvenile justice system is built on a racist foundation of criminalizing black children.
3. The current state of the juvenile justice system is a pipeline to adult criminal justice involvement for black children.

I propose that we advocate for the reallocation of funds from juvenile court to transform and reimagine what juvenile justice should be. The expenditure by municipalities to fund professional court staff and expensive juvenile detention centers simply does not reflect the needs of the communities that they serve. For instance, in the state of California, taxpayers spent an average of $284,700 to keep a child locked up in a juvenile hall in 2018. Once the cost of probation officials, administrative, and maintenance costs were added, the city of San Francisco's annual price to incarcerate **one** youth was $374,000. Several Bay Area counties were among those spending the most per child. The county of Santa Clara showed an annual cost of $531,400 to detain one youth in detention.[147]

Similarly, in fiscal year 2017, the city of Baltimore, Maryland, allocated 25.8 percent of its annual budget to police departments, according to the report, Freedom to Thrive: Reimagining Safety & Security in Our Communities. Community activists there have long maintained that the city under-invests in community based services for youth and over-invests in policing and incarceration.[148]

Reallocating funds from a more punitive juvenile justice purpose to a more holistic one such as diversion and community-based treatment is not a novel idea. For example, in San Francisco, a majority of the city's 11 supervisors, introduced legislation in 2019 to shut down the county's juvenile hall by the end of 2021 in order to create small, community-based alternatives, including a scaled-down secure facility for serious offenders.[149]

In 2019, the Governor also shifted the California Department of Corrections and Rehabilitation (CDCR) to the Health and Human Services Agency in order to address juvenile justice as a matter of public health. In a surprise move in the midst of the COVID-19 crisis, the Governor of California demanded an end to California's youth prison system.[150] Although juvenile crime rates have decreased significantly in the last decade, the cost of housing one youth in the juvenile system was significant. A portion of the cost savings as a result of these changes will be redirected to county probation departments, who will supervise youth in the community. Dan Macallair, executive director of the San Francisco-based Center on Juvenile and Criminal Justice, called the closure of these facilities an end to a '19th century system of juvenile justice,' and maintained that all of the children currently in juvenile justice custody could and should be supervised in the community.[151]

One of the most forward-thinking examples of reallocating funds from a juvenile justice system has occurred in Washington State. In 2017, the King County Executive directed that a multi-department team, led by the King County Public Health Department, adopt a public health approach to juvenile justice in order to limit the traumatization of youth in detention and to ensure that families have access to support and services in the community.[152] King County defines a public health approach to juvenile justice as 'engaging communities and applying a strong evidence base to determine prevention and intervention strategies that eliminate the need for juvenile detention and promote well-being and development of all youth.'[153] The approach is science-based and trauma-informed. The county funds community partners to provide services to youth and their families. The five objectives of the public health strategy are laudable and include strategies to achieve the objectives, goals, and continuing action items. The first objective is to lead with racial equity.[154]

The county celebrated the opening of a new children and family justice center in Seattle, Washington in March of 2020.[155] Although the center has some of the features of a typical juvenile justice system, it has some new and innovative features such as judges' benches that are lower and not as imposing as regular courtroom benches. Attorneys and defendants sit at single curved tables before the court and there is free childcare available and on-site. But, most importantly, the building has

100 fewer juvenile detention beds and the average daily population count reduced from 38 to 4 in a year.[156] In 1999, the average daily juvenile jail population in King County was 200 – most of them children of color. Derrick Wheeler Smith, the director of Zero Youth Detention at the King County Department of Health, said. "You can't invest in the future without divesting ourselves of the past."[157]

Delinquent

Daphne R. Robinson

Afterword

Much of what I've said in this book is not new or novel. But, it's taken me years of working in the juvenile justice system to put what I think is needed to re-envision the juvenile justice system in these pages. I know that this is not a complete list and I know that many working in the system and those looking in from the outside will disagree with me. But, these are my truths, not theirs. I don't regret my years as a prosecutor assigned to juvenile court. In some ways, I think it is why I was put on this earth. It has been a labor of the heart. It hasn't always been glamorous work or even work that I enjoyed, but it has been work that I committed myself to doing with integrity, fairness, and honesty. People have often asked me why I chose to remain in the shadows of the juvenile court prosecuting children rather than the spotlight that comes with prosecuting adults. My response to that is a great quote by Frederick Douglass, African-American abolitionist and statesman. Douglass said, "It is easier to build strong children, than to repair broken men." I hope that I have helped to build lots of strong children.

Delinquent

Daphne R. Robinson

About the Author

Daphne Robinson is a native of Greenville, Mississippi, a town in the Mississippi Delta. She is a graduate of Tougaloo College in Jackson, Mississippi and the American University Washington of Law in Washington, D.C. She

Daphne R. Robinson

completed her Master's Degree in Public Health with a concentration in Prevention Sciences from Emory University Rollins School of Public Health in Atlanta, Georgia.

Daphne has served as a prosecutor for more than 20 years in three jurisdictions in Louisiana and is currently the Executive Director of the Center for Public Health & Justice, a non-profit organization focused on improving the lived experience of people in the Mississippi Delta. She is also an adjunct professor of public health at Louisiana State University in Shreveport, Louisiana.

Endnotes

[1] Mississippi Delta. (2020, July 16). Retrieved July 16, 2020, from https://en.wikipedia.org/wiki/Mississippi_Delta

[2] Spitz, A. M. (1993, December 17). Surveillance for Pregnancy and Birth Rates Among Teenagers, by State -- United States, 1980 and 1990. Retrieved July 17, 2020, from https://www.cdc.gov/mmwr/preview/mmwrhtml/00031562.htm

[3] Wright, A. E. (2019, August 01). Teen pregnancy rate declines but remains high in the Delta; report says social and economic factors key to further reduction. Retrieved July 17, 2020, from https://mississippitoday.org/2019/07/31/teen-pregnancy-rate-declines-but-remains-high-in-delta-region-report-says-socioeconomic-factors-key-to-further-reduction/

[4] Alexander, M. (2020). The new Jim Crow: Mass incarceration in the age of colorblindness. New York, NY: New Press.

[5] M. Clair & Denis, J. S. (2015). Sociology of Racism. In N. J. Smelser (Author), International Encyclopedia of the Social & Behavioral Sciences (2nd ed., Vol. 19, pp. 12720-12723). Amsterdam, DE: Elsevier.

[6] Racial Disproportionality and Disparity in Child Welfare. (2016, November). Retrieved July 17, 2020, from https://www.childwelfare.gov/pubs/issue-briefs/racial-disproportionality/

[7] Alexander, M. (2020).

[8] Kendi, I. (2020, June 24).

[9] PBS. (1998). Africans in America | Part 1 | Narrative | From Indentured Servitude to Racial Slavery. Retrieved July 18, 2020, from https://www.pbs.org/wgbh/aia/part1/1narr3.html

[10] What Was it Like to be a Child Slave in America in the Nineteenth Century? n.d. Retrieved July 18, 2020 fromhttps://www.nationalarchives.gov.uk/documents/education/childhood-slavery-contextual-essay.pdf

[11] *ibid.*

[12] *ibid.*

[13] Children and Youth in History. (2010). Retrieved July 18, 2020, from http://chnm.gmu.edu/cyh/

[14] What Was it Like to be a Child Slave in America in the Nineteenth Century? n.d. Retrieved July 18, 2020 from https://www.nationalarchives.gov.uk/documents/education/childhood-slavery-contextual-essay.pdf

[15] *ibid.*

[16] *ibid.*

[17] Mullins, Melissa Ann, "Born into Slavery: The American Slave Child Experience" (1997). Dissertations, Theses, and Masters Projects. Paper 1539626128. https://dx.doi.org/doi:10.21220/s2-w1w7-8b19

[18] Beard, R. (2012, August 16). Lincoln's Panama Plan. Retrieved July 20, 2020, from https://opinionator.blogs.nytimes.com/2012/08/16/lincolns-panama-plan/

[19] Ward, G. K. (2012). *The Black Child-Savers: Racial Democracy and Juvenile Justice.* Chicago: The University of Chicago Press.

[20] Oshinsky, D. M. (1997). *"Worse than slavery": Parchman Farm and the Ordeal of Jim Crow Justice.* New York, NY: Free Press Paperbacks published by Simon & Schuster.

[21] Bragg, K., & Lewis, M. (2019, November 14). Bound by Statute. *Mississippi Today.* Retrieved July 18, 2020, from https://mississippitoday.org/2019/11/14/bound-by-statute-in-mississippi-jim-crow-era-laws-result-in-a-high-rate-of-black-kids-charged-as-adults/

[22] PICKETT, R. (1969). House of Refuge: Origins of Juvenile Reform in New York State, 1815-1857. Syracuse, New York: Syracuse University Press. doi:10.2307/j.ctv64h7hd

[23] Jackson, A. (2016, April 19). Repairing the Breach: A Brief History in the Justice System. Retrieved July 20, 2020, from https://www.burnsinstitute.org/publications/repairing-the-breach-pdf/

[24] *ibid.*

[25] ibid.

[26] Robin W. Sterling, Fundamental Unfairness: In re Gault and the Road Not Taken, 72 Md. L. Rev. 607 (2013) http://digitalcommons.law.umaryland.edu/mlr/vol72/iss3/1
[27] *ibid.*
[28] Agyepong, T. E. (2018). *The Criminalization of Black Children Race, Gender, and Delinquency in Chicago's Juvenile Justice System, 1899-1945.* Chapel Hill, NC: University of North Carolina Press.
[29] *ibid.*
[30] *iibid.*
[31] *ibid.*
[32] *ibid.*
[33] *ibid.*
[34] *ibid.*
[35] *ibid.*
[36] About Race Forward. (2020, June 01). Retrieved July 21, 2020, from https://www.raceforward.org/about
[37] *ibid.*
[38] Gee, G., & Ford, C. (2011, April 15). STRUCTURAL RACISM AND HEALTH INEQUITIES: Du Bois Review: Social Science Research on Race. Retrieved July 21, 2020, https://www.cambridge.org/core/journals/du-bois-review-social-science-research-on-race/article/structural-racism-and-health-inequities/014283FE003DFD8EF47A3AD974C72690
[39] Rovner, J. (2016, April 01). Racial Disparities in Youth Commitments and Arrests. Retrieved July 21, 2020, from http://www.sentencingproject.org/publications/racial-disparities-in-youth-commitments-and-arrests/
Rovner, J. (2016, April 01). Racial Disparities in Youth Commitments and Arrests. Retrieved July 21, 2020, from http://www.sentencingproject.org/publications/racial-disparities-in-youth-commitments-and-arrests/
[40] Black Disparities in Youth Incarceration. (2017, September 12). Retrieved July 21, 2020, from https://www.sentencingproject.org/publications/black-disparities-youth-incarceration/
[41] *ibid.*

[42] U.S. Census Bureau QuickFacts: United States. (n.d.). Retrieved July 21, 2020, from https://www.census.gov/quickfacts/fact/table/US/PST045219

[43] Michaels, S. (2017, September 13). Black Kids Are 5 Times Likelier Than White Kids to Be Locked Up. Retrieved July 21, 2020, from http://www.motherjones.com/politics/2017/09/black-kids-are-5-times-likelier-than-white-kids-to-be-locked-up/

[44] Civil Rights Data. (2020, January 10). Retrieved July 21, 2020, from https://www2.ed.gov/about/offices/list/ocr/data.html

[45] George, D. (2012, March 06). Federal data show racial gaps in school arrests. Retrieved July 21, 2020, from https://www.washingtonpost.com/national/federal-data-show-racial-gaps-in-school-arrests/2012/03/01/gIQApbjvtR_story.html

[46] *ibid.*

[47] The Social-Ecological Model: A Framework for Prevention |Violence Prevention|Injury Center|CDC. (2020, January 28). Retrieved July 21, 2020, from https://www.cdc.gov/violenceprevention/publichealthissue/social-ecologicalmodel.html

[48] *ibid.*

[49] Burns, B. et al. (2003, March). Treatment, Services, and Intervention Programs for Children. Retrieved July 21, 2020, from https://www.ncjrs.gov/pdffiles1/ojjdp/193410.pdf

[50] Denton, J. (2019, February 13). After Parkland, Schools Upped Police Presence. Has it Made Students Safer? - Justice Policy Institute. Retrieved July 21, 2020, from http://www.justicepolicy.org/news/12467

[51] *ibid.*

[52] American Psychological Association Zero Tolerance Task Force. (2008, December). Are zero tolerance policies effective in the schools?: An evidentiary review and recommendations. Retrieved July 21, 2020, from https://www.ncbi.nlm.nih.gov/pubmed/19086747

[53] Insley, Alicia C. "Suspending and Expelling Children from Educational Opportunity: Time to Reevaluate Zero Tolerance

Policies." American University Law Review 50, no. 4 (2001): 1039-1074.

54 Curran, F. (2019, February 14). Just what are 'zero tolerance' policies – and are they still common in America's schools? Retrieved July 21, 2020, from https://phys.org/news/2019-02-tolerance-policies-common-america-schools.html

55 Porter, N. (2013). Drug-Free Zone Laws: An Overview of State Policies. Retrieved July 21, 2020, from https://www.sentencingproject.org/wp-content/uploads/2015/12/Drug-Free-Zone-Laws.pdf

56 The Southern Poverty Law Center. (2019, June 16). The Data Gap: School policing in Louisiana. Retrieved July 21, 2020, from https://www.splcenter.org/20190616/data-gap-school-policing-louisiana

57 Justice Policy Institute. (2011, November). Education Under Arrest: The Case Against Police in Schools - Justice Policy Institute. Retrieved July 21, 2020, from http://www.justicepolicy.org/research/3177

58 Hutchinson, B. (2019, October 1). More than 30,000 children under age 10 have been arrested in the US since 2013: FBI. Retrieved July 21, 2020, from https://abcnews.go.com/US/30000-children-age-10-arrested-us-2013-fbi/story?id=65798787

59 Tooey, G. (2020, February 24). CRIME NEWS NEWS Body camera video: 6-year-old girl cries, screams for help as Orlando police arrest her at school. Orlando Sentinel.

60 ibid.

61 ACLU. (2017, April 12). Bullies In Blue: Origins and Consequences of School Policing. Retrieved July 21, 2020, from https://www.aclu.org/report/bullies-blue-origins-and-consequences-school-policing

62 Hutchinson, B. (2019, October 1). More than 30,000 children under age 10 have been arrested in the US since 2013: FBI. Retrieved July 21, 2020, from https://abcnews.go.com/US/30000-children-age-10-arrested-us-2013-fbi/story?id=65798787

63 ibid.

Daphne R. Robinson

Daphne R. Robinson

Daphne R. Robinson

Retrieved July 21, 2020, from
https://www.urban.org/sites/default/files/publication/99044/co
llecting_and_using_data_for_prosecutorial_decisionmaking_0
.pdf

[78] *ibid.*

[79] *ibid.*

[80] *ibid.*

[81] *ibid.*

[82] Edley, C., Jr. (2019, May 1). Toxic stress and children's outcomes. Retrieved July 22, 2020, from https://www.epi.org/blog/toxic-stress-and-childrens-outcomes

[83] Shonkoff JP;Garner A. (2012, January). The lifelong effects of early childhood adversity and toxic stress. Retrieved July 22, 2020, from https://pubmed.ncbi.nlm.nih.gov/22201156/

[84] CDC. (2020, April 13). About the CDC-Kaiser ACE Study |Violence Prevention|Injury Center|CDC. Retrieved July 22, 2020, from https://www.cdc.gov/violenceprevention/acestudy/about.html

[85] Baglivio. (2018, September 27). The Prevalence of Adverse Childhood Experiences (ACE) in the Lives of Juvenile Offenders. Retrieved July 22, 2020, from https://nicic.gov/prevalence-adverse-childhood-experiences-ace-lives-juvenile-offenders

[86] CDC. (2020, April 13).

[87] *ibid.*

[88] *ibid.*

[89] Baglivio. (2018, September 27).

[90] *ibid.*

[91] *ibid.*

[92] Goodman, R. A., & Hoffman, R. E. (2007). *Law in public health practice.* New York, NY: Oxford University Press.

[93] *ibid.*

[94] *ibid.*

[95] National Academies of Sciences, Engineering, & Medicine, (2017, January 11). The Root Causes of Health Inequity. Retrieved July 22, 2020, from https://www.ncbi.nlm.nih.gov/books/NBK425845/

[96] CDC. (2020, January 28). The Social-Ecological Model: A Framework for Prevention |Violence Prevention|Injury Center|CDC. Retrieved July 22, 2020, from https://www.cdc.gov/violenceprevention/publichealthissue/social-ecologicalmodel.html

[97] Child Welfare Information Gateway. (2016). Racial Disproportionality and Disparity in Child Welfare. Retrieved July 22, 2020, from https://www.childwelfare.gov/pubs/issue-briefs/racial-disproportionality/

[98] *ibid.*

[99] *ibid.*

[100] *ibid.*

[101] RFK National Resource Center for Juvenile Justice. (2014, May 8). From Conversation to Collaboration: How Child Welfare and Juvenile Justice Agencies Can Work Together to Improve Outcomes for Dual Status Youth. Retrieved July 22, 2020, from http://www.modelsforchange.net/publications/539

[102] *ibid.*

[103] *ibid.*

[104] Alexander, M. (2020). *The new Jim Crow: Mass incarceration in the age of colorblindness.* New York, NY: New Press.

[105] CDC. (2020, January 28).

[106] Institute of Medicine (US) Committee on Prevention of Mental Disorders. (1994, January 01). Risk and Protective Factors for the Onset of Mental Disorders. Retrieved July 22, 2020, from https://www.ncbi.nlm.nih.gov/books/NBK236306/

[107] Garland, D. (2001, January 1). Introduction: The Meaning of Mass Imprisonment - DAVID GARLAND, 2001. Retrieved July 22, 2020, from https://journals.sagepub.com/doi/10.1177/14624740122228203

[108] Wagner, W. (2020, March 24). Mass Incarceration: The Whole Pie 2020. Retrieved July 22, 2020, from https://www.prisonpolicy.org/reports/pie2020.html

[109] Gramlich, J. (2019, April 30). The gap between the number of blacks and whites in prison is shrinking. Retrieved August 12, 2020 from https://www.pewresearch.org/fact-

tank/2019/04/30/shrinking-gap-between-number-of-blacks-and-whites-in-prison/

[110] P.. Amato, L., Bonczar, T., Braman, D., L.. Bumpass, H., Comfort, M., K.. Edin, T., . . . B.. Western, J. (1995, January 01). Parental imprisonment, the prison boom, and the concentration of childhood disadvantage. Retrieved July 22, 2020, from https://link.springer.com/10.1353/dem.0.0052

[111] *ibid.*

[112] *ibid.*

[113] Wildeman, C. (2010, September 01). Paternal Incarceration and Children's Physically Aggressive Behaviors: Evidence from the Fragile Families and Child Wellbeing Study. Retrieved July 22, 2020, from https://academic.oup.com/sf/article-abstract/89/1/285/2235254

[114] *ibid.*

[115] Alexander, M. (2020).

[116] Hoffmann, E. (2015, March 06). How Incarceration Infects a Community. Retrieved July 22, 2020, from https://www.theatlantic.com/health/archive/2015/03/how-incarceration-infects-a-community/385967/

[117] *ibid.*

[118] Drucker, E. M. (2013). *A plague of prisons: The epidemiology of mass incarceration in America.* New York, NY: The New Press.

[119] *ibid.*

[120] Harvard University Center on the Developing Child. (2018, October 23). Resilience. Retrieved July 22, 2020, from https://developingchild.harvard.edu/science/key-concepts/resilience/

[121] Mental Health America. (n.d.). Protective and Risk Factors for Toxic Stress. Retrieved July 22, 2020, from https://mhanational.org/protective-and-risk-factors-toxic-stress

[122] Torres, N. (2019, November 01). Nurse-Family Partnership. Retrieved July 22, 2020, from https://www.blueprintsprograms.org/nurse-family-partnership/

[123] *ibid.*

[124] Miller, C. (2017, July 25). How Home Visits by Nurses Help Mothers and Children, Especially Boys. Retrieved July

22, 2020, from
https://www.nytimes.com/2017/07/25/upshot/how-home-visits-by-nurses-help-mothers-and-children-especially-boys.html

[125] Heckman, J. An Analysis of the Memphis Nurse-Family Partnership Program. (2017, October 17). Retrieved July 22, 2020, from https://heckmanequation.org/resource/analysis-memphis-nurse-family-partnership-program/

[126] Miller, C. (2017, July 25).

[127] Hill, Peggy MS Uris, Patricia PhD, RN, APRN Bauer, Tamar JD. (2007, November). Policy and Politics: The Nurse–Family Partnership: A Policy Priority. Retrieved July 22, 2020, from
https://www.nursingcenter.com/journalarticle?Article_ID=751232

[128] National Research Council. (1993),"Losing Generations: Adolescents in High-Risk Settings" at NAP.edu. (n.d.).

[129] Cohen, M., & Piquero, A. (2008, July 02). Benefits and Costs of a Targeted Intervention Program for Youthful Offenders: The Youthbuild USA Offender Project. Retrieved July 22, 2020, from
https://papers.ssrn.com/sol3/papers.cfm?abstract_id=1154055

[130] Mark A. Cohen, A. (2009, October 8).

[131] *ibid.*

[132] *ibid.*

[133] *ibid.*

[134] National Research Council. (1993),"Losing Generations: Adolescents in High-Risk Settings" at NAP.edu. (n.d.). Retrieved July 22, 2020, from
https://www.nap.edu/read/2113/chapter/13

[135] Hirsi, I., & Boyd, C. (2012, February 02). Project Spirit offers homework help and a lot more for African-American children in St. Paul school. Retrieved July 22, 2020, from
https://www.minnpost.com/community-sketchbook/2010/10/project-spirit-offers-homework-help-and-lot-more-african-american-child/

[136] Hirsi, I., & Boyd, C. (2012, February 02). Project Spirit offers homework help and a lot more for African-American

children in St. Paul school. Retrieved July 22, 2020, from https://www.minnpost.com/community-sketchbook/2010/10/project-spirit-offers-homework-help-and-lot-more-african-american-child/

[137] Hirsi, I., & Boyd, C. (2012, February 02). Project Spirit offers homework help and a lot more for African-American children in St. Paul school. Retrieved July 22, 2020, from https://www.minnpost.com/community-sketchbook/2010/10/project-spirit-offers-homework-help-and-lot-more-african-american-child/

[138] Zimmerman, M., Stoddard, S., Eisman, A., Caldwell, C., Aiyer, S., & Miller, A. (2013, December 1). Adolescent Resilience: Promotive Factors That Inform Prevention. Retrieved July 22, 2020, from https://www.ncbi.nlm.nih.gov/pmc/articles/PMC3839856/

[139] Lambert, E. (2020, June 09). Plan to remove police from Prince George's County Public Schools passes the first step.

[140] The Center for Restorative Approaches. (n.d.). Retrieved July 22, 2020, from http://www.thecra.net/

[141] National Juvenile Justice Network. (September, 2017). Implicit Bias. Retrieved August 03, 2020, from http://www.njjn.org/our-work/implicit-bias-snapshot

[142] The Ohio State University Kirwan Institute for Race and Ethnicity. (n.d.). Retrieved July 22, 2020, from http://kirwaninstitute.osu.edu/

[143] JESKE, J., & KLAS, M. (2016). Adverse Childhood Experiences: Implications for Family Law Practice and the Family Court System. Family Law Quarterly, 50(1), 123-137. Retrieved July 22, 2020, from www.jstor.org/stable/44155200

[144] *ibid.*

[145] Dierkhising, C. (2013, July 16). Trauma histories among justice-involved youth: Findings from the National Child Traumatic Stress Network. Retrieved July 22, 2020, from https://www.tandfonline.com/doi/full/10.3402/ejpt.v4i0.20274

[146] Tucker, J., & Palomino, J. (2020, February 25). Vanishing Violence: Cost of locking up a youth in California doubles, data show. Retrieved July 22, 2020, from https://www.sfchronicle.com/news/article/Vanishing-Violence-Cost-of-locking-up-a-youth-in-13793488.php

[147] *ibid.*

[148] Freedom to Thrive: Reimagining Safety & Security in Our Communities. (2020, June 17). Retrieved July 23, 2020, from https://populardemocracy.org/news/publications/freedom-thrive-reimagining-safety-security-our-communities?org=1312

[149] Tucker, J., & Palomino, J. (2020, February 25).

[150] Kushmaro, L. (2019, April 10). Reorganization of the Division of Juvenile Justice. Retrieved July 22, 2020, from https://lao.ca.gov/Publications/Report/3998

[151] Loudenback, J., Kelly, J., & Writer, G. (2020, May 15). In Surprise, Newsom Calls for an End to California's Youth Prison System. Retrieved July 22, 2020, from https://chronicleofsocialchange.org/justice/juvenile-justice-2/in-surprise-move-newsom-calls-for-an-end-to-californias-youth-prison-system/43366

[152] Constantine, D. (2017). News. Retrieved July 22, 2020, from https://www.kingcounty.gov/elected/executive/constantine/news/release/2017/November/16-juvenile-detention.aspx

[153] *ibid.*

[154] King County Public Health. (n.d.). King County Zero Youth Detention. Retrieved July 24, 2020, from https://kingcounty.gov/depts/health/zero-youth-detention.aspx

[155] Seattle, J. (2019, December 03). County's new Judge Patricia H. Clark Children and Family Justice Center is complete but don't expect a celebration anytime soon. Retrieved July 22, 2020, from https://www.capitolhillseattle.com/2019/12/countys-new-judge-patricia-h-clark-children-and-family-justice-center-is-complete-but-dont-expect-a-celebration-anytime-soon/

[156] Seattle, J. (2019, December 03). County's new Judge Patricia H. Clark Children and Family Justice Center is complete but don't expect a celebration anytime soon. Retrieved July 22, 2020, from https://www.capitolhillseattle.com/2019/12/countys-new-judge-patricia-h-clark-children-and-family-justice-center-is-complete-but-dont-expect-a-celebration-anytime-soon/

Delinquent

[157] *ibid.*

www.ingramcontent.com/pod-product-compliance
Lightning Source LLC
Chambersburg PA
CBHW071145090426
42736CB00012B/2233